LAZY &
EASY
ENGLISH

超効率的！

笑って覚える
イラスト
英単語

ジェイミー・チェイス 著

朝日出版社

Lazy & Easy English © 2008 by Jamie Chase
Japanese translation rights © 2011 by Asahi Press

All rights reserved. No part of this publication may be reproduced, stored in a retrieval system, or transmitted in any form, or by any mean (electronic, mechanical, photocopying, recording or otherwise) without the prior written permission of the copyright owner and the publisher of this book.

Printed in Japan

はじめに

　この本は、非英語圏の人たちが英語を学習するときに直面する、2つの大きな問題を解決することに重点を置いています。

　1つ目の問題は、耳と口が連動していない――リスニングとスピーキングが連動していないこと。2つ目は、なかなか単語を覚えられないこと、覚えてもすぐに忘れてしまうことです。

　「耳と口が連動していない」という問題を解決するためには、リスニングをしながら、その場面を頭の中でイメージすることから始める必要があると私は考えています。この本では、イラストを見ながら短い英文を聴いて学習します。そうすることによって、読者が耳で聴きながら英語で考えられるように導き、同時にイラストの裏ページに掲載されたテキストを目で読むことで英語での会話表現能力を効率的に向上させていきます。また、それぞれの単語の意味を理解しながら、文の中での正しい使い方を学ぶことになるので、自然と英語の文法が身につくようになります。

　次の「単語を覚えられない」という問題を解決するためには、これまでに学んだ単語を活用するのが近道です。すでに知っているやさしい単語をベースに、その単語と似ている単語を連係させて、「基本の単語」と「基本の単語と似ている新しい単語」を1つの文で使うようにするのです。この方法は、

新しい単語を覚えるのにとても役立ちます。知っている言葉と関連させることで新しい単語を早く覚えることができ、簡単には忘れにくくなります。

　さらにイラストを見ることで、英文が聴き取りやすく、そして理解しやすくなり、文中に出てくる新しい単語も忘れにくくなります。

　この本は、中学・高校・大学などの学生はもとより、約1,500個の基本単語（日本では高校1年までに習う）を知っている人であれば、年齢と関係なく誰でも学習することができます。

　どうか皆さんが、私のイメージ通りにこの本をうまく活用して、志を成し遂げられますように、心より願っています。

ジェイミー・チェイス

Contents

はじめに		3
この本の特長		6
学習の注意点		7
この本の効果的な使い方		8
プロローグ　英語はやさしく学べる！		10

Day 1	[CD track 01-09]	15
Day 2	[CD track 10-18]	35
Day 3	[CD track 19-27]	55
Day 4	[CD track 28-36]	75
Day 5	[CD track 37-45]	95
Day 6	[CD track 46-54]	115
Day 7	[CD track 55-63]	135
Day 8	[CD track 64-72]	155
Day 9	[CD track 73-81]	175
Day 10	[CD track 82-90]	195

Index & 単語チェック表	215

この本の特長

自分だけの「英語環境」を作る！

　非英語圏の人がうまく英語を話せないでいる環境において、英語を簡単に学ぶには、そのための理想的な「自分だけの英語環境」を作る必要があります。これは、実際に英語圏の国で生きているようにたくさんの英語を聴きながら、より身近に英語を学ぶことができる環境のことです。そうした理想的な環境を作るために、本書ではさまざまな工夫を凝らしています。

その1　笑えるマンガで、楽しくリスニング

　子供の頃に、英語圏の国へ移住した人たちと同じような方法で英語を学ぶことで、読者は必要以上の苦労をしなくても、英単語と文法を自然に結びつけることができます。イラストをよく観察しながら、その状況を理解できるようなきっかけを探すことが大事です。

その2　似た単語をまとめて体で覚える！

　本書では、単語を簡単に覚えられるように、つづりや発音が似た英単語で例文が作られています。生きた英単語を学ぶことになるので、単語が「無用なデータ」として周期的に頭の中で消去されることがなくなります。

その3　耳で聴いて、言葉で表現する力を鍛える

　新しい単語の正しい使用法を身につけながら、「耳」で聴いて理解する能力と、「言葉」で表現する能力を短期間に向上させることができます。無意識のうちに、話す内容を英語で考えられるように導いていきます。

その4　英語を習う時間がない人にも！

　本書は試験のための本ではなく、英語でコミュニケーションをとるための本です。年齢に関係なく、英語を学ぶすべての人々の助けとなり、特に「英語を使わなければならないのに習う時間がない」という人々にとっては大いに役立つでしょう。

学習の注意点

1. リラックスして学習する

学習するときは必要以上に身構えず、気軽な気持ちでリラックスして向かうといいでしょう。シャワーを浴びてからソファで楽にして学習してもかまいません。

2. 学習時間は30分以内に

勉強時間は30分を超えないこと。それ以上勉強すると、脳がデータを受け入れることを拒否し始めるためです。2～3回に分けて10～15分ずつ学習すればさらに効率的です。

3. 根気を持って取り組もう

この本は魔法の杖ではないので、ほんの数日間で英語の実力が奇跡的に高まるものではありません。しかし、長期的に考えると、この本が役立つことは明らかです。

この本の効果的な使い方

> 音声を聴く前には、解説を絶対に読まないように注意！

Step 1
イラストを見ながら、CDを聴く

該当するCDトラックの音声を聴いてみて、理解できないときはもう一度聴く。
3回聴いてもわからない場合には、Step 2に進む。

Step 2
解説を確認する

イラストの裏ページにある解説を読み、自分が理解した内容と合っているかどうかを確認する。

＜CDのトラック番号＞
● 各トラックに4つの例文の音声が収録されています。

＜キーワード＞
● 例文の中の、つづりや発音が似た単語が表記されています。

＜イラスト＞
● イラストを見ながら、CDの音声を聞き取ります。

Step 3
繰り返し声に出して読む

CDの音声を真似して、繰り返し声に出して読み、英語のフレーズを覚える。CDの音声と同じくらい流暢に言えるようになるまで、繰り返し練習する。

Step 4
復習する

何日間か時間を置いて、学習したフレーズがよく理解できていないと感じられるときは、復習する。

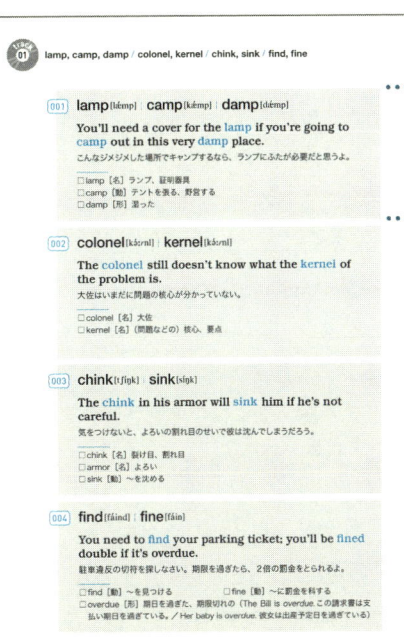

＜解説＞
● キーワードとその発音記号
● 英文および、その日本語訳
● 重要な語句とその意味

CDについて

この本に出てくるすべての例文が、**ネイティブの音声**で録音されています。Day1、3、5、7、9は**アメリカ英語**、Day 2、4、6、8、10は**イギリス英語**の音声が収録されています。

 プロローグ　英語はやさしく学べる！

●アジア人がぶつかる「英語の壁」

　ずいぶん前から、アジアにおける英語学習への取り組みは、非常に熱心です。しかし、数年間英語を学んでも、英語でコミュニケーションをとれない人がなんと多いことでしょうか。これは本当におかしな話です。アジア人はコンピュータや医学などの先端科学分野では優れた才能を発揮しているのに、それよりはるかにやさしく思える英語の学習で、つまずいてしまうのは一体なぜでしょうか。

　英語を学ぶことは、他の学問を学ぶのとはずいぶん勝手が違います。明確な定義づけがあり、いくつかの決まった法則を理解すればよい数学などとは異なり、英語は膨大な数の単語とその発音を覚えなければなりません。さらに難しいのは、単語をフレーズの中で正しく使うための規則が、必ずしも論理的な法則にもとづいていない点です。こうした理由から、アジア地域の多くの学生たちは英語を学ぶことに挫折し、英語の学習を阻む壁──"English Ceiling（英語の天井）"があるようだと口をそろえて言います。

　彼らは英語で話しかけられたり、英語のテレビ番組を見ても、教科書で習ったいくつかのフレーズ以外は理解できません。分かるのは、英語を全く習わなかった人でも聞き取れる"Thank you"や"Sorry"のような、ごく簡単なフレーズだけです。スピーキングに至っては、聴くことよりもはるかに難しく、口を開くたびに無力感を味わうことになります。

　また、英語を読むことも頭の痛い問題です。英語の教材は読めても、英字新聞や雑誌は分からない単語だらけで読み進めることができません。結局、分厚い英和辞典を開いて、単語を一つ一つ調べていくしかないのですが、そ

こまで大変な思いをして読み進めても、1時間以上かけてほとんど進んでいないことに気がつくと、放り出したくなります。しかも、この英文読解をしながら語彙力を増やす方法は、ほとんど効果がありません。なぜなら、せっかく覚えた単語も、数日たつと忘れてしまうからです。

こうしてアジアの学生たちの多くは、努力して何年も英語を勉強しても、大した成果も得られずに、ため息をつくことになるのです。

●アジアの英語教育は、ピアノを理論だけで習うようなもの

アジアの学校では、単語と文法を教えることから始め、その後、読み書きを学習するというのが一般的な英語教育法です。英語で考えたり、話したりする訓練はしません。生徒たちは、数学を勉強するのと同じように、本の上だけで英語を学びます。これは言ってみれば、ピアノを習うときに鍵盤にさわらずに、楽譜だけでピアノを練習しようとするようなものです。英語の教師たちはいわば、音楽理論だけを教えるピアノの先生のような存在です。

なぜこうした指導方法がとられるのか、その理由は簡単です。教師たち自身が、学生時代にそのようにして英語を習ってきたからです。教師たち自身が英語で考えることをせず、英語をたくさん話すこともできず、耳と口が連動していない――つまり、リスニングとスピーキングが頭の中で連動していないために、英語でコミュニケーションをとる方法を教えることができないのです。当然、そのような「耳と口をふさいだまま」の教育方法で、学生たちが英語でコミュニケーションをとれるはずがありません。

● 3000個の基本的な単語

　英語を日常的に使わない非英語圏の国で生活する学習者にとっては、英単語の中でも「最も基本的な3,000個」（日本の高校修了程度）を記憶するだけでもやっかいなことです。そして、それ以上の単語を覚えようとしても、簡単に忘れてしまいます。これでは、英語で自由にコミュニケーションをとるには明らかに不都合が生じます。学習者は苦労しながらも、3,000個の「基本的な単語」をどうにか暗記します。それが可能なのは、これらの「基本的な単語」が多くの英文の中に繰り返し現れるためです。しかし、それ以上の単語になると、英文の中で使われる頻度がガクンと下がるために、覚えるのが容易ではなくなります。

　英文の中に繰り返して現れる頻度が減ると、新しい単語を暗記するのは、「とうもろこし畑の熊」のように難しくなります。とうもろこし畑で、熊はとうもろこしを1つ取って片方のわきの下にはさみ、また1つ取っては反対側のわきの下にはさむという行動を繰り返しますが、新しいとうもろこしを取ったとき、すでにわきに挟んだとうもろこしが地面に落ちます。こうして熊がとうもろこしを何度取っても、そのたびに落としてしまうので、結局熊のわきの下には最後にはさんだとうもろこしが2本だけ残ることになります。残念なことに、アジアの学習者がよく陥るのは、まさにそれと同じような状態なのです。学習者は数日前に習った単語を覚えては忘れ、そこへさらに新しい単語を覚えようと努力します。しかし、新たに暗記した単語は、何日か過ぎればほとんど忘れられてしまいます。時間をかけて、それを何度繰り返してみても、いくら熱心に暗記しても、同じことです。ネズミが回し車をクルクルと回るように単語を暗記し続け、次々と忘れていってしまうのです。

　結局、そのうち頭の中に残っているのは、最近覚えたいくつかの単語だけで、多くの時間と労力を注いで暗記した他の単語は思い出せません。人間の脳では、「役に立たない」データを保存する空間が限られているため、脳は本能的に利益になるものを探し、不必要なものは避けるのです。

　したがって、「役に立たない」データの量が限られた空間を上回ると、脳は自動的にそのデータを消去し、「記憶したい」という人間の主観的な欲求は無視します。そして、どんなにたくさんの単語を覚えようと、いくら努力をしようと、日常生活において英語で考えたり話したりしなければ、脳の中に入っているその単語は「役に立たない」データと見なされ、定期的に削除されていきます。学習者たちの多くが「最も基本的な3,000語」を超える単語を記憶できない理由が、まさにここにあるのです。

● 「非英語圏」で英語を学ぶには？

　それでは、アジアの学習者が英語を簡単に身につけるには、どうすればいいのでしょうか。ここで、英語が分からない子供が、英語圏に移住した場合のことを考えてみましょう。

　移住した子供は、英語をまったく理解できません。未知の言語の中に放り出され、その子供は突然言葉を失います。しかし、日常生活の中で英語をたくさん聴くことで、何週間か後にはいくつかの簡単な英語のフレーズを話し始め、数カ月が過ぎると、聴いて理解する能力と言葉で表現する能力が飛躍的に高まります。そして1年が過ぎる頃には、その子が日常生活において表現できない言葉はほとんどなくなります。さらに、話し方や発音は現地の子供たちと変わらなくなり、自分の両親の発音のまちがいを指摘し始めます。

　英語で読むことができる文章の量はまだ多くありませんが、その子が英語のネイティブスピーカーでないと言う人はいないでしょう。このことは、英語を学ぶことは「聴くこと」から「話すこと」へと移行する過程であることを意味します。誰かが教えてくれるわけでもなく、その子供はただ、人が話すのを真似しながら、頭の中に自分が理解した単語のデータベースを着実に構築していきます。そして、保存された単語が8,000個以上になったとき、苦労せずに自然に英語を話せるようになります。

　毎日会話ができる英語のネイティブスピーカーがいれば、英語を学ぶのはさほど難しくありません。単語の意味や発音を習うことができるだけでなく、文の中での単語の使い方も学ぶことができるためです。そうすることによって、無意識のうちに頭の中に正しい英語の文法が蓄積されていくのです。当然ながら、こうした形で覚える単語はすべて、頭の中のデータベースに肯定的に保存されて、脳はその単語を「役に立つ」データとして認知するので、忘れることがありません。こうしたことから、言語を学ぶのは「記憶力」より、「真似る能力」の問題といえます。

　このように英語を学ぶときに最も重要なのは、日常生活の中で英語を十分に「聴く」ことであるのに、残念ながらアジアの学習者は、英語を十分に聴く機会がありません。まさにそれが、この地域の多くの学生たちが英語を学びにくくしている原因です。

　これまで述べてきたように、英語を身近に学ぼうとするなら、英語を使う環境が用意されるべきです。どうすればそのような環境を用意できるのでしょうか。この本はまさに、そのような環境を用意するために考案されたものです。

Day 1

Keywords for Day 1

- **01** lamp, camp, damp / colonel, kernel / chink, sink / find, fine
- **02** lamp, lump / mad, mud / lout, flout / emperor, empire
- **03** adopt, adapt / insist, resist / blind, blink / grill, frill
- **04** draft, drought / inventor, investor / crash, clash / instinct, distinct
- **05** beam, bean / breed, brood / convert, revert / release, lease
- **06** banner, ban / bust, bus / eel, heel / cast, castle
- **07** buck, luck / bulb, bulk / admission, permission / persist, insist
- **08** luck, duck, deck / blank, bland / cease, decease / decent deceit
- **09** battery, batter / envy, envoy / ledger, ledge / evade, invade

絵を見ながら Listen to the English!
発音やつづりが似た単語を、まとめて体で覚えよう！

001 lamp camp damp

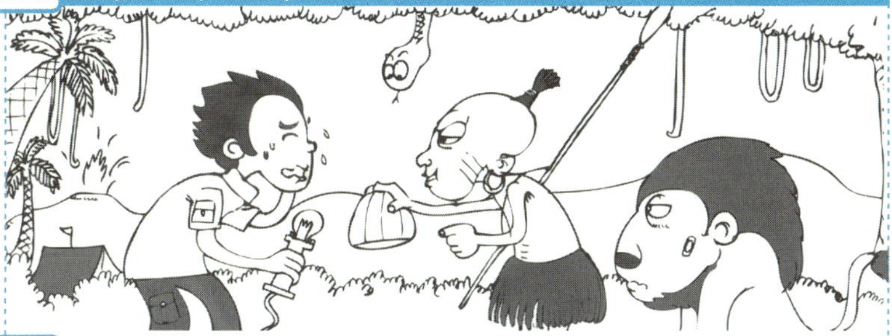

002 colonel kernel

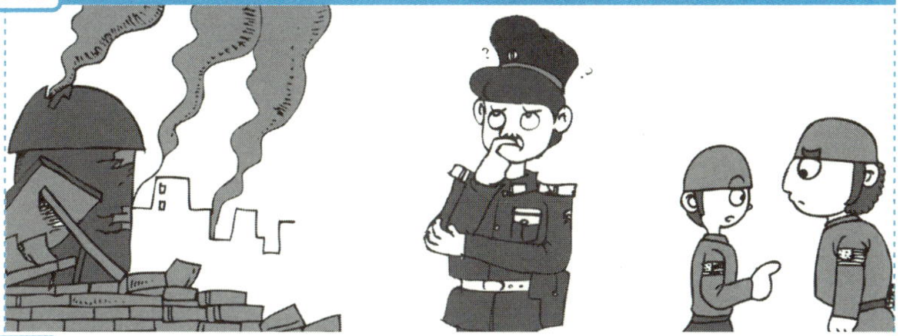

003 chink sink

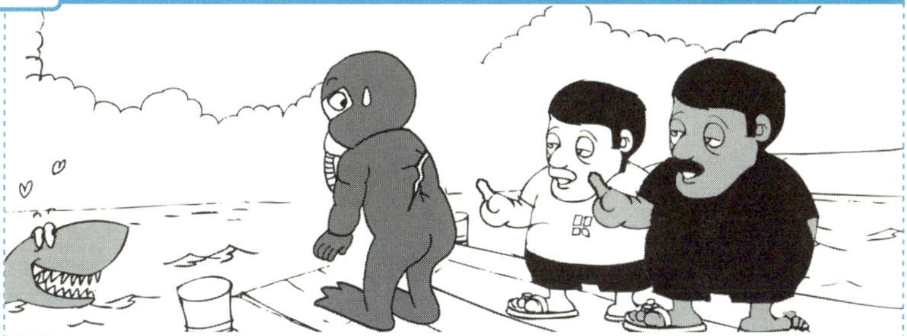

004 find fine

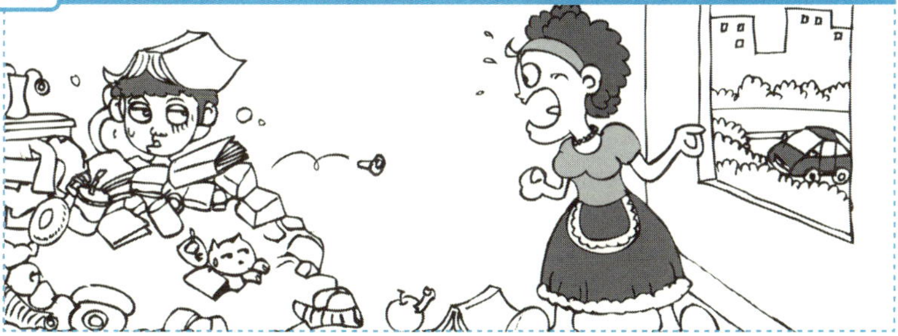

Day 1

lamp, camp, damp / colonel, kernel / chink, sink / find, fine

001 lamp [lémp] | camp [kémp] | damp [démp]

You'll need a cover for the lamp if you're going to camp out in this very damp place.

こんなジメジメした場所でキャンプするなら、ランプにふたが必要だと思うよ。

□ lamp［名］ランプ、証明器具
□ camp［動］テントを張る、野営する
□ damp［形］湿った

002 colonel [kə́ːrnl] | kernel [kə́ːrnl]

The colonel still doesn't know what the kernel of the problem is.

大佐はいまだに問題の核心が分かっていない。

□ colonel［名］大佐
□ kernel［名］（問題などの）核心、要点

003 chink [tʃíŋk] | sink [síŋk]

The chink in his armor will sink him if he's not careful.

気をつけないと、潜水服の割れ目のせいで彼は沈んでしまうだろう。

□ chink［名］裂け目、割れ目
□ armor［名］潜水服、よろい
□ sink［動］〜を沈める

004 find [fáind] | fine [fáin]

You need to find your parking ticket; you'll be fined double if it's overdue.

駐車違反の切符を探しなさい。期限を過ぎたら、2倍の罰金をとられるよ。

□ find［動］〜を見つける　　　□ fine［動］〜に罰金を科する
□ overdue［形］期日を過ぎた、期限切れの（The bill is overdue. この請求書は支払い期日を過ぎている。／ Her baby is overdue. 彼女は出産予定日を過ぎている）

Day 1

005 lamp　lump

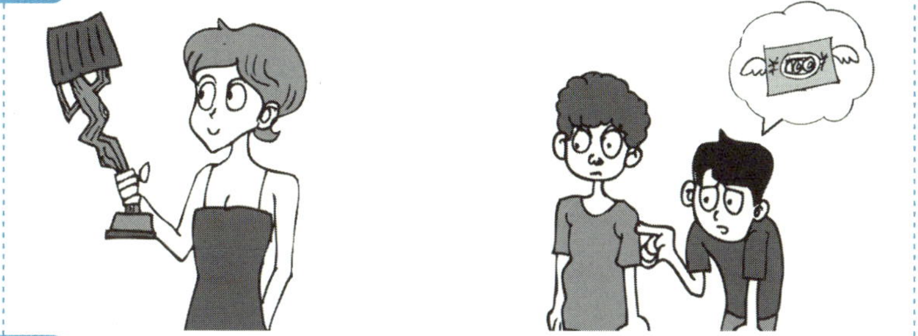

006 mad　mud

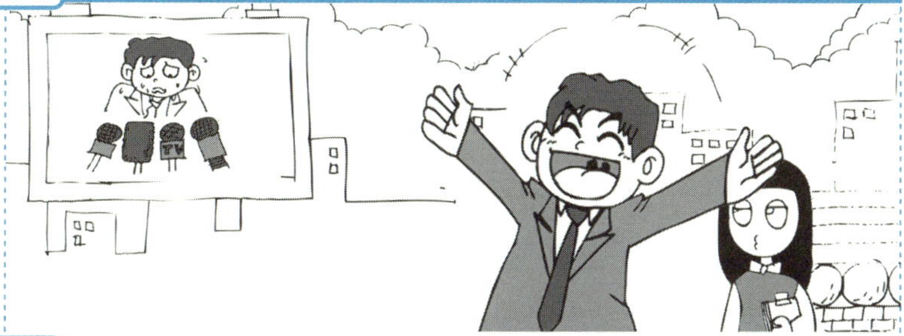

007 lout　flout

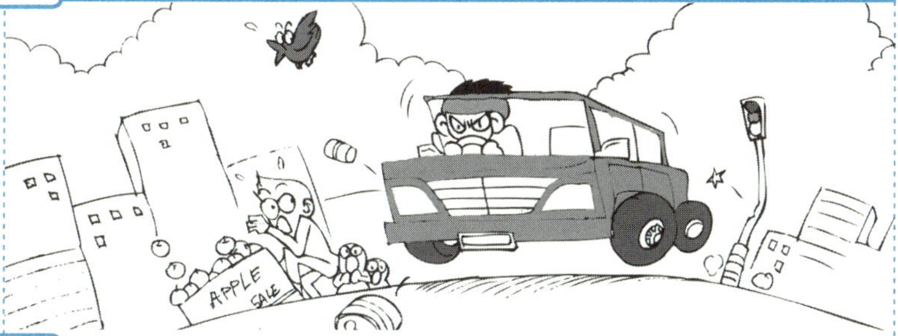

008 emperor　empire

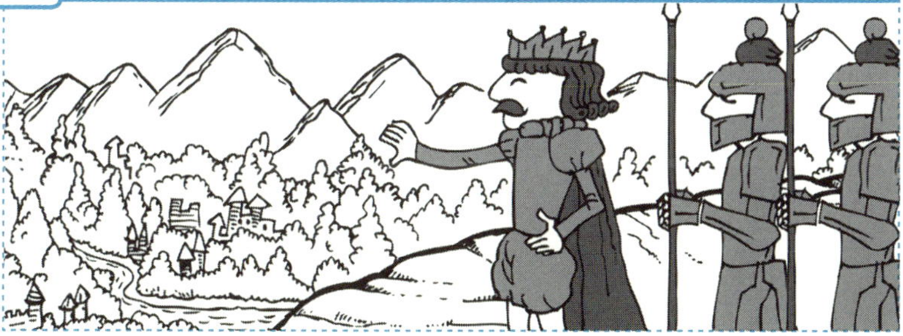

lamp, lump / mad, mud / lout, flout / emperor, empire

005 lamp [lǽmp] | lump [lʌ́mp]

She paid $100 for that lamp with the lumps.

彼女はこぶのついたランプに100ドル支払ったんだぜ。

- □ lamp [名] ランプ、証明器具
- □ lump [名] こぶ、塊 / □ take one's lumps 罰や報いを受ける

006 mad [mǽ(:)d] | mud [mʌ́d]

He ran around mad with joy when he saw that his opponent's name was mud.

敵の評判が地に落ちたのを見て、彼は小躍りして喜んだ。

- □ mad [形] 気が狂って / □ be mad with joy 狂喜する
- □ mud [名] つまらないもの、泥 / □ One's name is mud. 〈人〉の評判が地に落ちる

007 lout [láut] | flout [fláut]

He's a lout; he always flouts the law.

彼は無骨者だ。いつも法を破っている。

- □ lout [名] 無骨者
- □ flout [動] （規則などを）ばかにして従わない（No one can *flout* the law and get away with it. 法を破って逃げおおせる人はいない）

008 emperor [émpərər] | empire [émpaiər]

I am the emperor of this empire.

私は、この帝国の皇帝だ。

- □ emperor [名] 皇帝、帝王
- □ empire [名] 帝国

絵を見ながら **Listen to the English!**
発音やつづりが似た単語を、まとめて体で覚えよう！

解説は次ページ

Day 1

009 adopt adapt

010 insist resist

011 blind blink

012 grill frill

adopt, adapt / insist, resist / blind, blink / grill, frill

009 adopt [ədápt] | adapt [ədǽpt]

We adopted this boy from overseas just last year, but he has already adapted to life here.

私たちは去年、海外からこの少年を養子にしたばかりだが、彼はすでにここの生活になじんでいる。

□ adopt［動］〜を養子にする
□ adapt［動］順応する

010 insist [insíst] | resist [rizíst]

If he insists that he loves you, how can you resist?

彼があなたを愛していると言うなら、抵抗できる？

□ insist［動］〜を強く主張する
□ resist［動］抵抗する

011 blind [bláind] | blink [blíŋk]

Did you know that even blind people have to blink?

目の不自由な人でも、まばたきする必要があるって知っていた？

□ blind［形］目の不自由な
□ blink［動］まばたきする

012 grill [gríl] | frill [fríl]

One dollar for a 100-percent beef grilled burger with no frills.

百パーセントまじりっ気なしの牛肉グリルバーガーが1ドル。

□ grill［動］〜を焼き網で焼く
□ frill［名］余分なもの、余計な飾り / □ with no frills　余計なサービスを省いた

絵を見ながら Listen to the English!
発音やつづりが似た単語を、まとめて体で覚えよう！

track 04　　　　　　　　　　　　　　　解説は次ページ

013 draft　drought

014 inventor　investor

015 crash　clash

016 instinct　distinct

Day 1
Day 2
Day 3
Day 4
Day 5
Day 6
Day 7
Day 8
Day 9
Day 10

23

draft, drought / inventor, investor / crash, clash / instinct, distinct

013 **draft**[drǽft | drɑ́ːft] | **drought**[dráut]

Sitting in the evening draft, she told me how all her draft horses had died in the drought.

彼女は座って夜風にあたりながら、自分の荷馬が干ばつですべて死んでしまったことを話してくれた。

- □ draft［名］風
- □ draft horse　荷車を引く馬
- □ drought［名］日照り、干ばつ

014 **inventor**[invéntər] | **investor**[invéstər]

The inventor was short of investors to support his project.

その発明家の事業を支援してくれる投資家が不足していた。

- □ inventor［名］発明家、考案者
- □ be short of　〜が不足している
- □ investor［名］投資家

015 **crash**[krǽʃ] | **clash**[klǽʃ]

After he crashed his father's car yesterday, they had a clash.

昨日、彼は父親の車をぶつけてしまい、その後二人はけんかした。

- □ crash［動］（自動車などを）ぶつける、〜をつぶす
- □ clash［名］衝突、戦闘

016 **instinct**[ínstiŋkt] | **distinct**[distíŋkt]

My instinct tells me that there is a distinct possibility that the big guy will win.

私の直感が、大きいほうの男が勝つ可能性がはっきりあると告げている。

- □ instinct［名］直感、本能
- □ distinct［形］明瞭な、はっきりと認識できる
- □ possibility［名］可能性

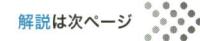

絵を見ながら Listen to the English!
発音やつづりが似た単語を、まとめて体で覚えよう！

| 017 | beam bean |

| 018 | breed brood |

| 019 | convert revert |

| 020 | release lease |

 Day 1
 Day 2
 Day 3
 Day 4
 Day 5
 Day 6
 Day 7
 Day 8
 Day 9

beam, bean / breed, brood / convert, revert / release, lease

017 beam [bíːm] | bean [bíːn]

Beaming with pride, she showed us the green **beans** growing in her garden.

彼女は誇らしげに微笑みながら、庭になっているサヤインゲンを私たちに見せてくれた。

- □ beam［動］微笑む、光を発する
- □ bean［名］豆

018 breed [bríːd] | brood [brúːd]

Pigeons **breed** often and are capable of having several **broods** each year.

ハトは頻繁に繁殖し、年に何度か卵を産むことができる。

- □ breed［動］繁殖する、子を産む
- □ be capable of 〜の能力がある
- □ brood［名］一かえりのひな、一腹の子

019 convert [kənvə́ːrt] | revert [rivə́ːrt]

We can **convert** coal to gas, but gas can't be **reverted** back into coal.

私達は石炭をガスに変化させることはできるが、ガスを石炭に戻すことはできない。

- □ convert［動］〜を変化させる、変換する
- □ coal［名］石炭
- □ revert［動］（元の状態に）戻る

020 release [rilíːs] | lease [líːs]

There is no way he is going to **release** you from this **lease**!

彼がこの賃貸借契約からあなたを解放してくれるわけがないでしょう！

- □ release［動］〜を解放する、自由にする
- □ lease［名］賃貸借契約

絵を見ながら **Listen to the English!**
発音やつづりが似た単語を、まとめて体で覚えよう！

解説は次ページ

Day 1

021 banner　ban

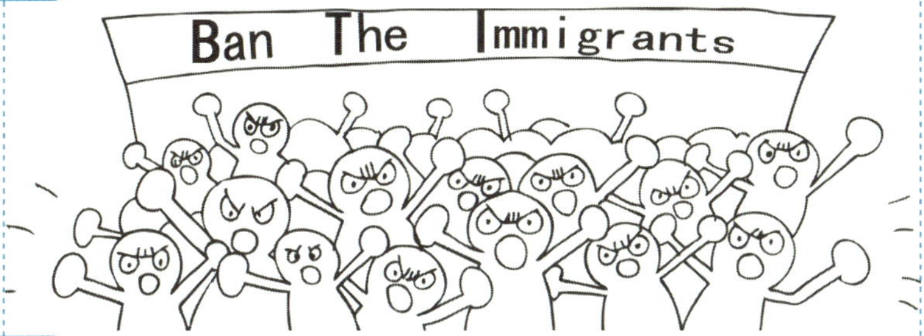

022 bust　bus

023 eel　heel

024 cast　castle

banner, ban / bust, bus / eel, heel / cast, castle

021 banner [bǽnər] | ban [bǽn]

Did you see the banner in the crowd yesterday that said, "Ban the immigrants!"

昨日、人ごみの中で「移民を禁止しろ！」という横断幕を見た？

- □ banner［名］横断幕、垂れ幕
- □ ban［動］〜を禁止する
- □ immigrant［名］移民、移住者

022 bust [bʌ́st] | bus [bʌ́s]

Wow! Check out the bust on that beauty waiting for the bus!

わお！ バスを待っている美人の胸を見ろよ！

- □ bust［名］胸部、バスト
- □ beauty［名］美人、美女
- □ bus［名］バス

023 eel [íːl] | heel [híːl]

Look! There's an eel under your heel!

ほら見て、君のハイヒールの下にうなぎがいるよ！

- □ eel［名］ウナギ
- □ heel［名］かかと、ハイヒール

024 cast [kǽst | kάːst] | castle [kǽsl | kάːsl]

Don't cast stones from the castle parapets!

城の胸壁から石を投げてはいけないよ！

- □ cast［動］〜を投げる、ほうる
- □ castle［名］城、城郭
- □ parapet［名］胸壁、(屋根などの) 手すり

28

絵を見ながら Listen to the English!
発音やつづりが似た単語を、まとめて体で覚えよう！

track 07

解説は次ページ

Day 1

| 025 | buck   luck |

| 026 | bulb   bulk |

| 027 | admission   permission |

| 028 | persist   insist |

buck, luck / bulb, bulk / admission, permission / persist, insist

025 buck [bʌk] | luck [lʌk]

If you pass the buck, you pass your luck as well.

責任を転嫁したら、運も手放してしまうことになるぞ。

- □ buck［名］ポーカーで次の配り番の前に置く札 / □ pass the buck　責任を転嫁する
- □ luck［名］運、成功

026 bulb [bʌlb] | bulk [bʌlk]

I always buy light bulbs in bulk.

私はいつも電球をまとめ買いする。

- □ bulb［名］電球、白熱灯 / □ light bulb　電球
- □ bulk［名］大量 / □ in bulk　まとめて

027 admission [ædmíʃən | əd-] | permission [pərmíʃən]

No admission without permission.

許可なしに入るべからず。

- □ admission［名］入ること、入場
- □ permission［名］許可、承認

028 persist [pərsíst] | insist [insíst]

If you persist in causing trouble, I'll insist you leave the room.

問題を起こすのをやめないなら、この部屋から出て行きなさい。

- □ persist in　〜に固執する
- □ insist［動］〜を強く主張する、言い張る

029 luck　duck　deck

030 blank　bland

031 cease　decease

032 decent　deceit

Day 1
Day 2
Day 3
Day 4
Day 5
Day 6
Day 7
Day 8
Day 9
Day10

luck, duck, deck / blank, bland / cease, decease / decent deceit

[029] **luck**[lʌ́k] | **duck**[dʌ́k] | **deck**[dék]

It was pure luck that I caught the duck on the deck of the boat.

船のデッキでカモを捕まえたのは幸運だった。

- □ luck ［名］幸運、運命（pure *luck* ただのまぐれ）
- □ duck ［名］カモ、アヒル
- □ deck ［名］（船の）デッキ、甲板

[030] **blank**[blǽŋk] | **bland**[blǽnd]

Without her, my days are as blank as this bland soup.

彼女なしでは、毎日がこの味の薄いスープのように空虚だ。

- □ blank ［形］空虚な、白紙の（If you press this key, the screen will go *blank*. このキーを押すと、画面情報が消える）
- □ bland ［形］味の薄い、味気ない

[031] **cease**[síːs] | **decease**[disíːs]

You can cease paying taxes after you are deceased, but not before.

死亡したら税金を払わなくてもよくなるが、それまでは払わなくてはならない。

- □ cease ［動］〜を止める、中止する / □ cease fire　停戦する
- □ decease ［動］死亡する / □ deceased ［形］死んだ、死亡した

[032] **decent**[díːsənt] | **deceit**[disíːt]

Decent people despise deceit.

まともな人はごまかしを嫌う。

- □ decent ［形］きちんとした、まともな、上品な
- □ despise ［動］〜を軽蔑する、嫌悪する
- □ deceit ［名］だますこと、ごまかし

絵を見ながら Listen to the English!
発音やつづりが似た単語を、まとめて体で覚えよう！

解説は次ページ

033 battery　batter

034 envy　envoy

035 ledger　ledge

036 evade　invade

Day 1
Day 2
Day 3
Day 4
Day 5
Day 6
Day 7
Day 8
Day 9
Day 10

battery, batter / envy, envoy / ledger, ledge / evade, invade

033 **battery** [bǽtəri] | **batter** [bǽtər]

We found a good battery in that old battered car.
あのボロ車には、いいバッテリーが積んであった。

□ battery ［名］バッテリー、電池
□ batter ［動］〜を連打する / □ battered ［形］傷んだ、ボロボロの

034 **envy** [énvi] | **envoy** [énvɔi]

I do envy the privileges he enjoys as a government envoy.
私は彼の政府特使として享受している特権がうらやましい。

□ envy ［動］〜をうらやむ、ねたむ
□ privilege ［名］特権、恩恵
□ envoy ［名］使節、外交官

035 **ledger** [lédʒər] | **ledge** [lédʒ]

The ledger is on the window ledge.
台帳はその窓台の上にありますよ。

□ ledger ［名］台帳
□ ledge ［名］出っ張り、棚（window *ledge* 窓台）

036 **evade** [ivéid] | **invade** [invéid]

He goes out of his way to evade the tourists who invade this summer resort each summer.
毎年夏になると、このサマーリゾートに押し寄せる観光客から逃れるために、彼は違う場所に行く。

□ go out of one's way 自分の道からそれる
□ evade ［動］〜を逃れる、避ける
□ invade ［動］〜に侵攻する、押し寄せる

Day 2

Keywords for Day 2

- **track 10** — fling, flint / bust, bus, robust / aide, aid / craft, raft
- **track 11** — flask, flash / decry, decoy / know, knot / lie, lay
- **track 12** — fussy, fuzzy / scrape, cape / cook, crook, look, took, hook / crawl, scrawl
- **track 13** — loss, lost / pick, brick / bead, bread / instance, stance
- **track 14** — cost, post, pose / bound, rebound / assure, reassure / lick, flick
- **track 15** — bask, ask / pick, pack / lack, black / beach, bleach
- **track 16** — bleak, leak / bleak, break / fleet, flee / slap, lap
- **track 17** — rave, cave / huge, hug / hostility, hospitality / hotel, motel, hostel
- **track 18** — compose, composition / slick, lick, lip / editor, edit, auditor, audit / bow, elbow

track 10 絵を見ながら **Listen to the English!**
発音やつづりが似た単語を、まとめて体で覚えよう！

解説は次ページ

037 fling flint

038 bust bus robust

039 aide aid

040 craft raft

fling, flint / bust, bus, robust / aide, aid / craft, raft

037 fling [flíŋ] | flint [flínt]

She did fling the flint at me, but luckily it missed me.

彼女は私に向かって火打ち石を投げつけたが、幸いにも当たらなかった。

- □ fling［動］〜を投げつける、放り出す
- □ flint［名］火打ち石

038 bust [bʌ́st] | bus [bʌ́s] | robust [roubʌ́st]

He went bust and sold his bus to a robust company.

彼は倒産し、活気のある会社にバスを売った。

- □ go bust　倒産する、つぶれる
- □ bus［名］バス
- □ robust［形］強固な、活気のある、堅固な（That chair is not very *robust*. あの椅子はあまり頑丈ではない）

039 aide [éid] | aid [éid]

The presidential aide asked for police aid in dealing with the demonstrators.

大統領の側近は、デモ隊に対処するために警察の援助を頼んだ。

- □ presidential［形］大統領の
- □ aid［名］援助、救援
- □ aide［名］補佐官、側近
- □ demonstrator［名］デモの参加者

040 craft [krǽft | krɑ́:ft] | raft [rǽft | rɑ́:ft]

We clambered into the rescue craft from our small life raft.

われわれは小さな救命ボートから、救助船によじ登った。

- □ clamber［動］よじ登る、はい上がる
- □ craft［名］船、飛行機、航空機 / □ rescue craft　救助船
- □ raft［名］いかだ、ゴムボート / □ life raft　救命ボート

track 11 絵を見ながら **Listen to the English!**
発音やつづりが似た単語を、まとめて体で覚えよう！

解説は次ページ

041 flask　flash

042 decry　decoy

043 know　knot

044 lie　lay

flask, flash / decry, decoy / know, knot / lie, lay

041 flask [flǽsk | flάːsk] | flash [flǽʃ]

She dropped the flask on the floor when the lightning flashed.

稲妻がピカッと光り、彼女は瓶を床に落としてしまった。

- □ flask ［名］フラスコ、瓶、《英》魔法瓶
- □ lightning ［名］稲妻、電光
- □ flash ［動］ピカッと光る、点滅する

042 decry [dikrái] | decoy [díːkɔi]

Many people decry the use of decoys.

デコイの使用を非難する人は多い。

- □ decry ［動］〜をけなす、（公然と）非難する
- □ decoy ［名］おとり用の鳥の模型、デコイ

043 know [nóu] | knot [nάt | nɔ́t]

She doesn't know how to knot a rope.

彼女はひもの結び方を知らない。

- □ know ［動］〜を知っている
- □ knot ［動］〜に結び目をつくる、〜を結ぶ

044 lie [lái] | lay [léi]

Lying down on the job is not allowed. Get back to work right now if you don't want to be laid off.

仕事の怠慢は許されないぞ。解雇されたくなければ、ただちに仕事に戻りなさい。

- □ lie down on the job　仕事をおろそかにする、任務をおこたる
- □ lay off　〜を一時解雇する

track 12 絵を見ながら **Listen to the English!**
発音やつづりが似た単語を、まとめて体で覚えよう！

解説は次ページ

045 fussy　fuzzy

046 scrape　cape

047 cook　crook　look　took　hook

048 crawl　scrawl

fussy, fuzzy / scrape, cape / cook, crook, look, took, hook / crawl, scrawl

[045] **fussy**[fʌ́si] | **fuzzy**[fʌ́zi]

She's very fussy and insisted on buying the washing machine with the fuzzy function.

彼女はとても気難しく、ファジー機能のある洗濯機を買うと言い張った。

- □ fussy［形］小うるさい、気難しい
- □ fuzzy［形］ファジーな、不明瞭な、あいまいな、不鮮明な（The TV picture is rather *fuzzy* tonight. 今夜はテレビの画面がなんだか不鮮明だな）

[046] **scrape**[skréip] | **cape**[kéip]

I'm going to scrape the mud off my cape now.

これから私はケープについた泥をこすり落とす。

- □ scrape off　〜をこすり落とす、削り取る（I *scraped* the skin *off* the potatos. 私はじゃがいもの皮をこすり落とした）
- □ mud［名］泥
- □ cape［名］ケープ、袖なしの肩マント

[047] **cook**[kúk] | **crook**[krúk] | **look**[lúk] | **took**[túk] | **hook**[húk]

That cook is a crook! Look! He is the one that took the meat from the hook!

あの料理人は泥棒だ！ ほら、留め金から肉を取ったのは彼だよ！

- □ cook［名］料理人、コック
- □ Look!　見て、ほら
- □ hook［名］留め金
- □ crook［名］いかさま師、悪党、泥棒
- □ take［動］〜を取る

[048] **crawl**[krɔ́:l] | **scrawl**[skrɔ́:l]

He crawled across the room and scrawled his dying words on the floor.

彼は部屋の中を腹ばいで進み、床の上に最期の言葉を書き記した。

- □ crawl［動］腹ばいで進む、はう
- □ scrawl［動］〜を走り書きする、殴り書きする

track 13 絵を見ながら **Listen to the English!**
解説は次ページ
発音やつづりが似た単語を、まとめて体で覚えよう！

049 loss lost

050 pick brick

051 bead bread

052 instance stance

Day 2

loss, lost / pick, brick / bead, bread / instance, stance

[049] **loss** [lɔ́(ː)s] | **lost** [lɔ́(ː)st]

It's a big loss for him to have lost his car.

車を失ったのは、彼にとって大きな損失だ。

☐ loss［名］失うこと / ☐ a big loss 大きな損害、大損
☐ lose［動］〜を失う、なくす（He *lost* all his property. 彼は財産をすべて失った）

[050] **pick** [pík] | **brick** [brík]

They picked up and carried by hand 5,000 bricks to build that wall.

彼らはあの壁を作るために、5千個のレンガを持ち上げて運ばなければならなかった。

☐ pick up 〜を持ち上げる、拾い上げる
☐ brick［名］レンガ

[051] **bead** [bíːd] | **bread** [bréd]

Would you swap your shiny beads for my bread?

君の光輝くビーズのネックレスを僕のパンと交換してくれないかい？

☐ swap［動］〜を交換する、取り換える
☐ shiny［形］光る、輝く
☐ bead［名］ビーズ、《~s》ビーズのネックレス
☐ bread［名］パン

[052] **instance** [ínstəns] | **stance** [stǽns | stάːns]

You can't depend on her at all. For instance, she has changed her stance on that issue twice already!

彼女はまったく頼りにならない。例えばこの件に関して、彼女はすでに2回も姿勢を変更しているんだ。

☐ instance［名］場合、事実、例 / ☐ for instance 例えば
☐ stance［名］姿勢、立場

絵を見ながら Listen to the English!

発音やつづりが似た単語を、まとめて体で覚えよう！

track 14 解説は次ページ

053 cost　post　pose

054 bound　rebound

055 assure　reassure

056 lick　flick

cost, post, pose / bound, rebound / assure, reassure / lick, flick

053 **cost** [kɔ́(ː)st] | **post** [póust] | **pose** [póuz]

The high cost of posting letters by express mail does pose a problem for the company.

速達で手紙を出すための高い費用は、会社にとって問題だ。

- □ cost［名］費用
- □ express mail　速達便
- □ post［動］《英》〜を郵送する
- □ pose［動］（問題を）引き起こす

054 **bound** [báund] | **rebound** [ribáund]

The ball is bound to come back to you as it rebounds off the wall.

そのボールは壁から跳ね返って、戻ってくるはずだ。

- □ be bound to　きっと〜する、確かに〜するはずだ
- □ rebound［動］跳ね返る

055 **assure** [əʃúər] | **reassure** [rìːəʃúər]

I can assure you that the bank will reassure the customers that their savings are safe.

銀行が顧客に対して、預金が無事だと安心させるだろうことは断言できる。

- □ assure［動］（人に）〜であると断言する、〜を保証する
- □ reassure［動］〜を安心させる、〜に再保証する

056 **lick** [lík] | **flick** [flík]

He licked the ice cream cone as he idly flicked through the magazine.

彼はぼんやりと雑誌のページをめくりながらアイスクリームコーンをなめた。

- □ lick［動］〜をなめる
- □ idly［副］これといった目的もなく
- □ flick［動］（ほこりなどを）払い落とす / □ flick through　（本を）パラパラめくる

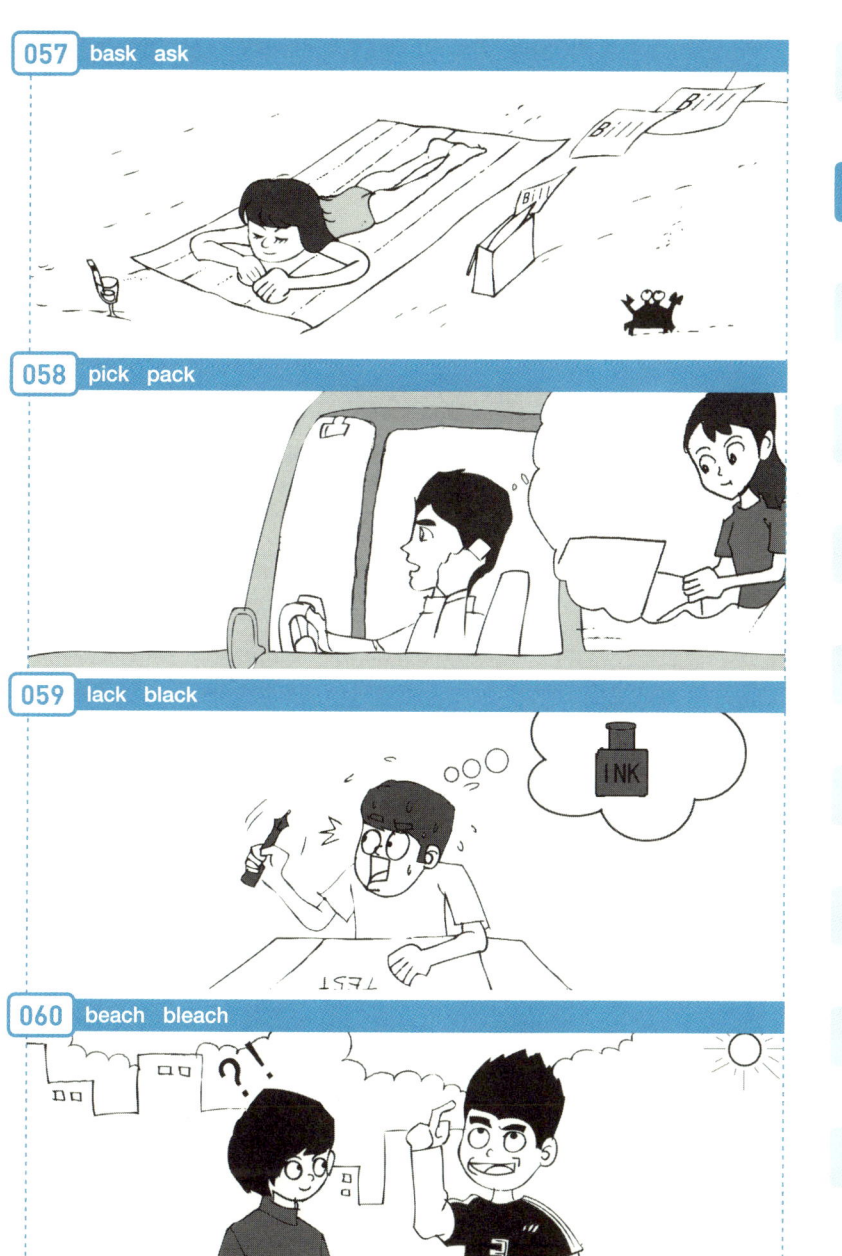

track 15 絵を見ながら **Listen to the English!**
解説は次ページ
発音やつづりが似た単語を、まとめて体で覚えよう！

| 057 | bask   ask |

| 058 | pick   pack |

| 059 | lack   black |

| 060 | beach   bleach |

bask, ask / pick, pack / lack, black / beach, bleach

[057] **bask**[bǽsk | bάːsk] | **ask**[ǽsk | άːsk]

Basking in the sunshine, she didn't feel like asking any questions at all.

日光浴をしながら、彼女はどんな質問もする気にならなかった。

□ bask ［動］日光に当たる、日光浴をする
□ ask ［動］〜を尋ねる

[058] **pick**[pík] | **pack**[pǽk]

I'll pick you up in 30 minutes, so pack your things up now.

30分後に車で迎えにいくから、すぐに荷物をまとめて。

□ pick up （人を）車で迎えに行く、車でひろう
□ pack up 荷物をまとめる、荷造りする

[059] **lack**[lǽk] | **black**[blǽk]

How could I lack black ink at a time like this?!

こんなときに黒インクがなくなるなんて！

□ lack ［動］（必要なものを）欠く
□ black ［形］黒い

[060] **beach**[bíːtʃ] | **bleach**[blíːtʃ]

I'll go to the beach to let the sun bleach my hair.

海辺に行って、日焼けして髪の色を抜くんだ。

□ beach ［名］海辺、浜
□ bleach ［動］〜を色あせさせる、漂白する

track 16 　絵を見ながら Listen to the English!
発音やつづりが似た単語を、まとめて体で覚えよう！

解説は次ページ

061 bleak　leak

062 bleak　break

063 fleet　flee

064 slap　lap

bleak, leak / bleak, break / fleet, flee / slap, lap

061 **bleak** [blíːk] | **leak** [líːk]

It's a bleak day; I knew that sooner or later someone would leak the story to the press.

今日は気がめいる日だ。遅かれ早かれ、誰かがマスコミにその話をもらすだろうことは分かっていた。

- □ bleak［形］（見通しなどが）暗い、気がめいるような
- □ leak［動］（秘密などを）漏らす、漏えいする

062 **bleak** [blíːk] | **break** [bréik]

The prospects for change in that country are bleak since no one has been able to break his hold on power.

誰も彼の政権を終わらせることができないので、あの国における改革の見通しは暗い。

- □ prospect［名］見通し
- □ bleak［形］（見通しが）暗い
- □ break［動］〜を終わらせる
- □ hold on power　権力にしがみつくこと

063 **fleet** [flíːt] | **flee** [flíː]

We won't let his fleet flee this time!

今回はやつの艦隊を逃がさないぞ！

- □ fleet［名］艦隊、海軍
- □ flee［動］逃げる、すばやく動く

064 **slap** [slǽp] | **lap** [lǽp]

She threatened to slap him if he tried to take the chocolate in her lap.

彼女は、膝の上のチョコレートを取ろうとしたらひっぱたくわよ、と彼を脅した。

- □ threaten［動］〜と脅す
- □ slap［動］〜をひっぱたく、平手打ちにする
- □ lap［名］ひざ

track 17 絵を見ながら Listen to the English!
発音やつづりが似た単語を、まとめて体で覚えよう！

解説は次ページ

065 rave　cave

066 huge　hug

067 hostility　hospitality

068 hotel　motel　hostel

rest house
auto court
hotel

Day 2

rave, cave / huge, hug / hostility, hospitality / hotel, motel, hostel

065 **rave**[réiv] | **cave**[kéiv]

He raved to God when he found he was trapped in the cave.
彼は洞窟の中に閉じ込められたと分かったとき、神に向かって夢中で話しかけた。

- □ rave［動］夢中になって話す、とりとめのないことを言う
- □ trap［動］（人を）閉じ込める
- □ cave［名］洞くつ、ほら穴

066 **huge**[hjúːdʒ | hjúːdʒ] | **hug**[hʌ́g]

She gave him a huge hug to celebrate his good luck.
彼の幸運を祝して、彼女は彼をギュッと抱きしめた。

- □ huge［形］非常に大きい
- □ hug［名］抱擁

067 **hostility**[hɑstíləti | hɔs-] | **hospitality**[hὰspətǽləti | hɔ̀s-]

I can see the hostility under his hospitality.
彼の手厚いもてなしの裏に、悪意を感じる。

- □ hostility［名］敵意、対立
- □ hospitality［名］手厚いもてなし、歓待

068 **hotel**[houtél] | **motel**[moutél] | **hostel**[hʌ́stl | hɔ́s-]

Would you prefer to stay at a hotel, a motel, or a hostel?
ホテルかモーテル、それかユースホステル、どこに泊まりたいですか？

- □ hotel［名］ホテル、旅館
- □ motel［名］モーテル、自動車旅行用の宿泊施設
- □ hostel［名］ユースホステル、簡易宿泊施設

絵を見ながら Listen to the English!
発音やつづりが似た単語を、まとめて体で覚えよう！

track 18

解説は次ページ

069 compose composition

070 slick lick lip

071 editor edit auditor audit

072 bow elbow

069 **compose**[kəmpóuz] | **composition**[kɑ̀mpəzíʃən | kɔ̀m-]

He composed his first musical composition when he was just 10.

彼は弱冠10歳のときに、最初の楽曲を作曲した。

☐ compose ［動］〜を作曲する、構成する
☐ musical composition　楽曲、音楽作品

070 **slick**[slík] | **lick**[lík] | **lip**[líp]

He was a slick fast talker who often licked his lips.

彼は早口で口先がうまく、よく唇をなめた。

☐ slick ［形］口のうまい、ペラペラとしゃべる
☐ lick ［動］〜をなめる / ☐ lick one's wounds　傷を癒す
☐ lip ［名］唇

071 **editor**[édətər] | **edit**[édit] | **auditor**[ɔ́ːdətər] | **audit**[ɔ́ːdit]

An editor edits books, while an auditor audits assets.

編集者は本を編集するが、会計検査官は資産を監査する。

☐ editor ［名］編集者、編集長　　　☐ edit ［動］〜を編集する
☐ auditor ［名］会計検査官　　　　☐ audit ［動］（会計を）検査をする
☐ asset ［名］資産、財産

072 **bow**[báu] | **elbow**[élbou]

I bowed to him, but he elbowed me out of the way.

私は彼におじぎをしたが、彼は私をひじで押しのけた。

☐ bow ［動］おじぎをする、会釈する
☐ elbow ［動］〜をひじで押す / ☐ elbow ... out of the way　ひじで（人を）押しのける

Day 3

Keywords for Day 3

- **track 19**: decent, accent / feat, feast / beat, beast, feast / able, ramble
- **track 20**: found, fount / bush, ambush / branch, ranch / erupt, corrupt
- **track 21**: expense, expanse / low, slow / perceive, conceive / lug, lung
- **track 22**: slug, lug / click, lick / bottom, button / lubricate, fabricate
- **track 23**: instinct, extinct / dumb, dump / dumb, dump / despite, respite
- **track 24**: outcome, income / bullet, pellet / debit, debt / bug, hug
- **track 25**: fudge, fridge / instance, instant / fag, flag / crack, rack
- **track 26**: pinch, inch / hoot, hook / maze, gaze / fury, fur
- **track 27**: construct, constrict / confidence, confide / restrict, constrict / tough, cough

track 19 絵を見ながら **Listen to the English!**
発音やつづりが似た単語を、まとめて体で覚えよう！

解説は次ページ

Day 3

073 decent　accent

074 feat　feast

075 beat　beast　feast

076 able　ramble

decent, accent / feat, feast / beat, beast, feast / able, ramble

073 decent [díːsənt] | accent [ǽksent]

She is a decent young lady with a lovely Irish accent.
彼女は美しいアイルランドなまりで話す、上品な娘さんです。

- □ decent［形］礼儀正しい、魅力的な
- □ lovely［形］美しい、かわいらしい
- □ Irish［形］アイルランドの
- □ accent［名］なまり、アクセント

074 feat [fíːt] | feast [fíːst]

What a feat to cater such a wonderful feast!
このような素晴らしい祝宴に料理の仕出しをするなんて、すごい芸当だ！

- □ feat［名］手柄、功績
- □ cater［動］〜に料理などを提供する
- □ feast［名］饗宴、ごちそう

075 beat [bíːt] | beast [bíːst] | feast [fíːst]

We'll beat the evil beast when it comes out to feast in the dead of the night.
真夜中、その邪悪な生き物が食事をしに出てきたときにやっつけよう。

- □ beat［動］〜をやっつける、殴打する
- □ beast［名］獣、動物
- □ in the dead of night 真夜中に
- □ evil［形］邪悪な、有害な
- □ feast［動］ぜいたくに食べる

076 able [éibəl] | ramble [rǽmbəl]

Tourists will be able to ramble around in space soon.
旅行者は近々、宇宙空間で散策することができるようになるだろう。

- □ be able to 〜することができる
- □ ramble［動］散歩する、ぶらつく（They *rambled* through the woods. 彼らは木々の間を散策した）

track 20 　絵を見ながら **Listen to the English!**
発音やつづりが似た単語を、まとめて体で覚えよう！

解説は次ページ

077　found　fount

078　bush　ambush

079　branch　ranch

080　erupt　corrupt

found, fount / bush, ambush / branch, ranch / erupt, corrupt

077 found [fáund] | fount [fáunt]

After I grew up, I found out that the old man was a fount of wisdom.

大人になってから、その老人が英知あふれる賢者だということに気づいた。

- find out 気がつく、発見する
- fount [名] 源、源泉
- wisdom [名] 英知、知恵（He's a man of great *wisdom*. 彼はすばらしい知恵をもった人物だ）

078 bush [búʃ] | ambush [ǽmbuʃ]

I'm not going to send my troops into the bush just to be ambushed!

私は自分の部隊を低木の茂みの中に配備したりしない。待ち伏せして攻撃されるのがオチだ。

- troop [名] 軍隊、中隊
- bush [名] 低木、茂み
- ambush [動] 〜を待ち伏せして攻撃する

079 branch [brǽntʃ | brάːntʃ] | ranch [rǽntʃ | rάːntʃ]

The bank refused to set up a branch at his ranch.

銀行は、彼の農場で支店を設けることを拒否した。

- refuse [動] 〜を断る
- branch [名] 支店、部門、枝
- ranch [名] 牧場、農場

080 erupt [irʌ́pt] | corrupt [kərʌ́pt]

Violence will erupt soon if the corrupt officials aren't arrested.

腐敗した当局者達が逮捕されなければ、近いうちに暴動が起きるだろう。

- violence [名] 暴力、暴力行為
- corrupt [形] 腐敗した、堕落した
- arrest [動] 〜を逮捕する
- erupt [動]（暴動などが）勃発する
- official [名] 当局者

絵を見ながら Listen to the English!
発音やつづりが似た単語を、まとめて体で覚えよう！

track 21
解説は次ページ

081 expense　expanse

082 low　slow

083 perceive　conceive

084 lug　lung

expense, expanse / low, slow / perceive, conceive / lug, lung

081 expense [ikspéns] | expanse [ikspǽns]

It was at great expense that we traveled through that expanse of land.

私達があの広大な土地を旅するには、莫大な費用がかかった。

- □ expense［名］費用、支出（It's too much of an *expense* to own a car. 車を所有するには費用がかかりすぎる）
- □ expanse［名］広がり、（空や大地などの）広々とした空間

082 low [lóu] | slow [slóu]

Put your car in low and drive slow when you see a Z sign.

Z字形の標識を見たら、ギアをローに入れてゆっくり走ってください。

- □ low［名］（自動車の）ローギア　［形］低い
- □ slow［副］ゆっくり、遅く
- □ Z sign　Z字形の標識、ジグザグ道の注意を呼び掛ける標識

083 perceive [pərsíːv] | conceive [kənsíːv]

The guard just happened to perceive that the prisoner had conceived a plan of escape.

囚人が逃亡の計画を抱いているということに、看守はたまたま気づいてしまった。

- □ perceive［動］（感覚で）〜に気づく
- □ conceive［動］（計画などを）思いつく、（考えなどを）抱く（I can't *conceive* why you told her. なぜ君が彼女に言ったのか、僕には全く想像できない）

084 lug [lʌg] | lung [lʌŋ]

I helped her lug her suitcase up the stairs because she has lung cancer.

彼女は肺がんを患っているから、荷物を持って階段を上がるのを手伝ったんだ。

- □ lug［動］（重いものを）苦労して運ぶ
- □ lung［名］肺 / □ lung cancer　肺がん

track 22 絵を見ながら **Listen to the English!**
発音やつづりが似た単語を、まとめて体で覚えよう！

解説は次ページ

085 slug　lug

086 click　lick

087 bottom　button

088 lubricate　fabricate

slug, lug / click, lick / bottom, button / lubricate, fabricate

085 slug [slʌ́g] | lug [lʌ́g]

It's nothing for a slug to lug itself up a wall.

壁をはい上がるなんて、ナメクジにとっては何でもないよ。

- □ slug［名］怠け者、ナメクジ
- □ lug［動］〜を苦労して運ぶ、引っ張りあげる

086 click [klík] | lick [lík]

I told you to click it, not lick it!

私はクリックするように言ったのよ、なめなさいとは言ってないわ！

- □ click［動］（マウスやアイコンを）クリックする、（ボタンを）カチッと押す
- □ lick［動］〜をなめる

087 bottom [bátəm | bɔ́t-] | button [bʌ́tn]

"Bottoms up!" he said. "Button up," she said.

「乾杯！」と彼が言った。「ボタンをとめて」と彼女は言った。

- □ bottom［名］下部、底 / □ Bottoms up!　乾杯！
- □ button［名］ボタン / □ button up　ボタンをとめる、黙る

088 lubricate [lúːbrəkèit] | fabricate [fǽbrikèit]

Yes, I have wined and dined some VIPs to lubricate business, but that story is totally fabricated.

ええ、確かに私はビジネスを円滑にするために、何人かのVIPを接待しました。でも、あの話は完全にでっち上げです。

- □ wine and dine　気前よくもてなす、酒を飲みながら食事する
- □ lubricate［動］〜を円滑にする
- □ fabricate［動］（話を）作り上げる

track 23 絵を見ながら **Listen to the English!**
発音やつづりが似た単語を、まとめて体で覚えよう！

解説は次ページ

089　instinct　extinct

090　dumb　dump

091　dumb　dump

092　despite　respite

Day 1
Day 2
Day 3
Day 4
Day 5
Day 6
Day 7
Day 8
Day 9
Day 10

65

instinct, extinct / dumb, dump / dumb, dump / despite, respite

089 **instinct**[ínstiŋkt] | **extinct**[ikstíŋkt]

Sex is a human instinct, otherwise we would be extinct by now.

セックスは人間の本能です。そうでなければ、われわれはとっくに絶滅していたでしょう。

- □ sex［名］性行為、性別
- □ instinct［名］本能、直感
- □ extinct［形］絶滅した

090 **dumb**[dʌ́m] | **dump**[dʌ́mp]

I can't believe that dumb guy could just dump his girlfriend like that.

あのバカな男が、あんなふうにガールフレンドを振るなんて信じられない。

- □ dumb［形］頭の悪い、まぬけな
- □ dump［動］（恋人を）振る、（中身を）どさっと放り出す

091 **dumb**[dʌ́m] | **dump**[dʌ́mp]

That dumb driver dumped a ton of mulch from his dump truck in the middle of my driveway!

あの頭の悪い運転手が、家の私道の真ん中に、ダンプカーから大量の根覆いを捨てやがった！

- □ dumb［形］頭の悪い、まぬけな
- □ mulch［名］根覆い
- □ driveway［名］（道路から家の車庫への）私道
- □ dump［動］〜をどさっと降ろす
- □ dump truck　ダンプカー

092 **despite**[dispáit] | **respite**[réspit | -pait]

She was still tired despite a few days respite.

2、3日の休息を取ったにもかかわらず、彼女はまだ疲れていた。

- □ despite［前］〜にもかかわらず（He remained modest *despite* his achievements. 彼は自らの偉業にもかかわらず、謙虚なままでいた）
- □ respite［名］息抜き、休息

track 24 絵を見ながら Listen to the English!
発音やつづりが似た単語を、まとめて体で覚えよう！

解説は次ページ

093 outcome　income

094 bullet　pellet

095 debit　debt

096 bug　hug

outcome, income / bullet, pellet / debit, debt / bug, hug

093 **outcome**[áutkʌm] | **income**[ínkʌm]

The outcome of the negotiations is that the income tax rate has been cut.

所得税率が削減されたことが、その協議の成果だ。

- outcome［名］結果、成果
- negotiation［名］交渉、協議
- income［名］所得、収入

094 **bullet**[búlət] | **pellet**[pélət]

A bullet is actually just a small lead pellet.

弾丸は、実はただの小さな鉛の球だ。

- bullet［名］弾丸、銃弾
- lead［形］鉛の
- pellet［名］小球、錠剤

095 **debit**[débit] | **debt**[dét]

Just debit that against my account, and I'll pay up the debt next time.

これはツケておいてよ。次回、耳をそろえて返すから。

- debit［動］（簿記で）～を借方に記入する
- account［名］勘定
- pay up　借金を全額払う
- debt［名］借金、負債

096 **bug**[bʌ́g] | **hug**[hʌ́g]

Please take care of that bug before you hug me.

私を抱きしめる前に、あの虫を始末してね。

- bug［名］虫、昆虫
- hug［動］～を抱きしめる、抱擁する

track 25 **絵を見ながら Listen to the English!**
発音やつづりが似た単語を、まとめて体で覚えよう！

解説は次ページ

097 fudge fridge

098 instance instant

099 fag flag

100 crack rack

Day 3

fudge, fridge / instance, instant / fag, flag / crack, rack

097 fudge [fʌdʒ] | fridge [frídʒ]

They tried to fudge the figures on the number of fridges they sold.

彼らは冷蔵庫の売上数をごまかそうとした。

□ fudge［動］〜をごまかす、でっち上げる（The figures on this report are *fudged.* この報告書の数字はごまかされている）
□ figure［名］数字
□ fridge［名］冷蔵庫（refrigeratorの短縮語）

098 instance [ínstəns] | instant [ínstənt]

Our service is the best. For instance, we can install an instant hot water system for you within a day.

私達のサービスは最高です。例えば、その日のうちに即席給湯システムを取り付けて差し上げられますよ。

□ instance［名］例、場合、事実 / □ for instance　例えば
□ install［動］〜を取り付ける、インストールする
□ instant［形］即席の、すぐの

099 fag [fæ(ː)g] | flag [flæ(ː)g]

I was fagged out after holding that big flag the whole morning.

午前中ずっとあの大きな旗を支えていたので、くたくたに疲れていた。

□ be fagged out　くたくたに疲れている、へとへとになる
□ flag［名］旗

100 crack [krǽk] | rack [rǽk]

We found a crack in the roof rack.

われわれは車の屋根の荷台に亀裂を見つけた。

□ crack［名］割れ目、ひび
□ roof rack《英》車の屋根の上の荷台

track 26 絵を見ながら **Listen to the English!**
発音やつづりが似た単語を、まとめて体で覚えよう！

解説は次ページ

101 pinch　inch

102 hoot　hook

103 maze　gaze

104 fury　fur

pinch, inch / hoot, hook / maze, gaze / fury, fur

101 pinch [pínt∫] | inch [ínt∫]

I won't let them pinch even one inch of our territory.
1インチたりとも、われらの領土を奪われないぞ。

- pinch［動］〜を盗む、横取りする（Somebody *pinch*ed my pen again! 誰かがまた僕のペンを盗ったよ！）
- inch［名］インチ
- territory［名］領土、領地

102 hoot [hú:t] | hook [húk]

He hooted with laughter when he learned that I hadn't hooked a fish all day.
僕が一日かけて魚を一匹も釣れなかったことを知ると、彼は笑いながらやじった。

- hoot［動］やじる（The audience *hoot*ed him off the stage. 観客はやじって、彼をステージから追い出した）
- hook［動］（魚を釣り針で）釣る

103 maze [méiz] | gaze [géiz]

When she told me she had lost her watch in the maze, she dared not meet my gaze.
迷路の中で時計をなくしたことを僕に伝えたとき、彼女は僕の視線を避けた。

- maze［名］迷路、迷宮
- dare［助動］思い切って…する
- gaze［名］凝視、じっと見つめること

104 fury [fjúəri] | fur [fə́:r]

She flew into a fury when I criticized her for wearing a real fur coat.
本物の毛皮のコートを着ていることを批判したら、彼女は激怒してしまった。

- fury［名］激怒、憤慨 / □fly into a fury 烈火のごとく怒る
- criticize ... for …を〜の理由で批判する
- fur［名］毛皮

track 27 絵を見ながら Listen to the English!
発音やつづりが似た単語を、まとめて体で覚えよう！

解説は次ページ

105 construct　constrict

106 confidence　confide

107 restrict　constrict

108 tough　cough

73

construct, constrict / confidence, confide / restrict, constrict / tough, cough

105 construct [kənstrʌ́kt] | constrict [kənstríkt]

It's difficult to construct an overall understanding of the situation if you have a constricted point of view.

視野が狭いと、全体的な状況に対する理解を構築するのは難しい。

- □ construct［動］〜を組み立てる、建設する
- □ overall［形］全体の
- □ constricted［形］抑制された

106 confidence [kɑ́nfədəns | kɔ́n-] | confide [kənfáid]

You'll need to win her confidence before she'll confide in you.

彼女があなたに秘密を打ち明けるためには、彼女の信頼を得る必要がある。

- □ win［動］〜を得る
- □ confidence［名］信頼、自信
- □ confide in 〜を信用する、〜を信用して秘密を打ち明ける

107 restrict [ristríkt] | constrict [kənstríkt]

The doctor said I had to restrict myself to two cigars a day, as smoking constricts the blood vessels.

喫煙は血管を収縮させるので、葉巻は1日2本に抑えなければならないと医者に言われた。

- □ restrict［動］〜を制限する、限定する
- □ constrict［動］〜を収縮させる、締めつける
- □ blood vessel　血管

108 tough [tʌ́f] | cough [kɔ́(ː)f]

You need to be tough so as not to catch a cold or a cough during the winter.

冬に風邪や咳風邪をひかないためには、体が丈夫でなくてはならないぞ。

- □ tough［形］強い、頑丈な
- □ cough［名］咳 / □ catch a cough　咳の風邪をひく

Day 4

Keywords for Day 4

track 28 backpacker, back, pack, backpack / infuse, infusion / fuse, defuse / conduct, deduct

track 29 inwards, outwards, forwards, backwards / evaluate, evacuate / executive, execute / knee, kneel

track 30 lower, glower / love, rove / flunk, fluke / both, botch

track 31 confirm, conform / confirmation, conformation / lash, slash / ditch, itch

track 32 brief, grief / gripe, grip / rope, grope / comb, tomb

track 33 sledge, edge / bump, bumper / aunt, jaunt / grain, grin

track 34 grin, grid / grid, grind / conscious, conscience / boaster, boast, booster

track 35 advertise, adverse / chop, chopper / explicit, implicit / fun, funky

track 36 clue, glue / restrict, district / emit, remit / fuse, refuse, defuse

絵を見ながら Listen to the English!
track 28
発音やつづりが似た単語を、まとめて体で覚えよう！

解説は次ページ

109 backpacker　back　pack　backpack

110 infuse　infusion

111 fuse　defuse

112 conduct　deduct

77

backpacker, back, pack, backpack / infuse, infusion / fuse, defuse / conduct, deduct

[109] **backpacker**[bǽkpæ̀kər] | **back**[bǽk] | **pack**[pǽk] | **backpack**[bǽkpæ̀k]

He's a backpacker from England. He's leaving today, so he ought to be back soon to pack his backpack.

彼はイギリスからのバックパッカーです。今日出発する予定だから、荷造りのためにすぐに戻ってくるはずよ。

- □backpacker［名］バックパッカー
- □pack［動］〜を詰め込む
- □back［副］戻って
- □backpack［名］リュックサック

[110] **infuse**[infjúːz] | **infusion**[infjúːʒən]

If you infuse the herbs in hot water for a few minutes, the infusion will be more effective.

この薬草を熱湯で2、3分煎じれば、浸出がより効果的になりますよ。

- □infuse［動］〜を煎じる、（人に信念や思想などを）吹き込む
- □infusion［名］浸出、（思想などの）注入
- □effective［形］効果的な

[111] **fuse**[fjúːz] | **defuse**[diː(ː)fjúːz]

You have to remove the fuse in order to defuse the bomb.

爆発の危険をなくすため、導火線を取り除かなくてはならない。

- □remove［動］〜を取り除く
- □fuse［名］導火線、信管
- □defuse［動］（爆発物の）信管を外す、（危険を）和らげる、鎮める

[112] **conduct**[kəndʌ́kt] | **deduct**[didʌ́kt]

If I don't need a guide to conduct me around, will you deduct $50 from the service charge?

案内してくれるガイドが必要なければ、サービス料から50ドル引いてもらえますか？

- □conduct ... around （人を）案内する
- □deduct［動］〜を差し引く、控除する
- □service charge　サービス料、手数料

絵を見ながら **Listen to the English!**
発音やつづりが似た単語を、まとめて体で覚えよう！

解説は次ページ

113 inwards outwards forwards backwards

114 evaluate evacuate

115 executive execute

116 knee kneel

Day 4

113 inwards [ínwərdz] | outwards [áutwərdz] | forwards [fɔ́ːrwərdz] | backwards [bǽkwərdz]

To play this game, you have to keep going inwards, outwards, forwards and backwards.
このゲームでは内側、外側、前方、後方に進み続けなければならないんだ。

- □ inward(s) ［副］内側に向けて
- □ forward(s) ［副］前方へ
- □ outward(s) ［副］外側へ
- □ backward(s) ［副］後方へ

114 evaluate [ivǽljuèit] | evacuate [ivǽkjuèit]

We must evaluate our ability to evacuate the local residents in case of an emergency.
われわれは、緊急時に地元の住民を非難させる能力があるか評価しなければならない。

- □ evaluate ［動］〜を評価する
- □ evacuate ［動］〜を避難させる
- □ resident ［名］居住者
- □ ability ［名］能力、才能
- □ local ［形］地元の
- □ emergency ［名］緊急事態

115 executive [igzékjutiv] | execute [éksikjùːt]

The executive's plan in itself was good, but somehow it was badly executed.
重役の計画そのものは優れていたが、どうしたものか実現の方法がまずかった。

- □ executive ［名］経営幹部、重役
- □ somehow ［副］どういうわけか
- □ execute ［動］〜を実行する

116 knee [níː] | kneel [níːl]

To lift the barbell, you first have to bend your knees and kneel down.
バーベルを持ち上げるには、まず、ひざを曲げて床につけなければいけない。

- □ bend ［動］〜を曲げる
- □ knee ［名］ひざ
- □ kneel down　ひざまずく、ひざをつく

絵を見ながら Listen to the English!
発音やつづりが似た単語を、まとめて体で覚えよう！

track 30

解説は次ページ

117 lower　glower

118 love　rove

119 flunk　fluke

120 both　botch

lower, glower / love, rove / flunk, fluke / both, botch

117 **lower**[lóuər] | **glower**[gláuər]

She lowered her head as he glowered at her.

彼がにらみつけると、彼女は頭を垂れた。

☐ lower ［動］〜を下げる、低くする
☐ glower at 〜をにらみつける

118 **love**[lʌ́v] | **rove**[róuv]

I love to rove the seas in search of adventure.

僕は冒険を求めて海をさまようのが好きだ。

☐ love to 〜するのが好きである
☐ rove ［動］〜を流浪する、さまよう
☐ in search of 〜を探し求めて
☐ adventure ［名］冒険

119 **flunk**[flʌ́ŋk] | **fluke**[flúːk]

He would have flunked out had he not passed the last exam by a fluke.

彼が最後の試験をまぐれで通っていなかったら、退学になっていただろう。

☐ flunk out （成績不良で）退学になる、試験に落第する
☐ fluke ［名］まぐれ、フロック（a *fluke* discovery 偶然の発見）

120 **both**[bóuθ] | **botch**[bɑ́tʃ]

We both tried our best to cook a nice dinner, but we really botched it.

私たちはおいしい食事を作ろうと最善を尽くしたけれど、大失敗してしまった。

☐ both ［代］両方ともに
☐ botch ［動］〜をしくじる、台無しにする（a *botched* job 失敗した仕事）

絵を見ながら Listen to the English!
発音やつづりが似た単語を、まとめて体で覚えよう！

解説は次ページ

121 confirm　conform

122 confirmation　conformation

123 lash　slash

124 ditch　itch

confirm, conform / confirmation, conformation / lash, slash / ditch, itch

121 confirm [kənfə́ːrm] | conform [kənfɔ́ːrm]

We have to confirm that this piece of equipment conforms to safety standards.

私達はこの装置が安全基準を満たしているかどうか、確かめなければならない。

- confirm [動] 〜を確認する
- conform [動] 従う、適合する、一致する (You must either *conform* to the rules or leave the school. 君は規則に従うか、さもなければ退学しなければならない)

122 confirmation [kɑ̀nfərméiʃən | kɔ̀n-] | conformation [kɑ̀nfɔːrméiʃən | kɔ̀n-]

We need your confirmation that this policy is in conformation with the new law.

この方針が新しい法律に則っていると、あなたに確認してもらうことが必要だ。

- confirmation [名] 確認、確証
- policy [名] 方針、政策
- conformation [名] 適合、一致 / be in conformation with 〜にかなって

123 lash [lǽʃ] | slash [slǽʃ]

He lashed out at the superintendent who had slashed the education budget by 30 percent.

彼は教育予算を30%削減した責任者を激しく非難した。

- lash out at 〜を厳しく非難する
- superintendent [名] (組織などの) 最高責任者、管理者
- slash [動] (予算・人員などを) 大幅に削減する

124 ditch [dítʃ] | itch [ítʃ]

Ever since I fell into that filthy ditch, I itch.

あの汚いどぶに落ちて以来ずっと、かゆいんです。

- filthy [形] 汚い、汚れた
- ditch [名] 溝、どぶ
- itch [動] かゆい、(〜したくて) むずむずする

track 32 絵を見ながら **Listen to the English!**
解説は次ページ
発音やつづりが似た単語を、まとめて体で覚えよう！

125 brief grief

126 gripe grip

127 rope grope

128 comb tomb

brief, grief / gripe, grip / rope, grope / comb, tomb

125 brief [bríːf] | grief [gríːf]

Life is so brief that I have no time for grief.

人生はあまりに短いので、私には悲しんでいる暇はない。

- □ so ... that 〜　あまりに…なので〜
- □ brief ［形］短時間の、簡潔な (a *brief* letter 短信、短い手紙)
- □ grief ［名］悲しみ、嘆き

126 gripe [gráip] | grip [gríp]

She always gripes about her father's firm grip on her.

彼女は父親の締めつけが厳しいことについて、いつも不平を言っている。

- □ gripe about　〜について不平を言う
- □ firm ［形］断固たる、力強い
- □ grip ［名］支配、握ること

127 rope [róup] | grope [gróup]

He tied his horse to the gate with a piece of rope and groped his way to the door in the darkness.

彼はロープで馬を門につないで、ドアまで暗闇の中を手探りで進んだ。

- □ rope ［名］縄、ロープ
- □ grope one's way　手探りして進む

128 comb [kóum] | tomb [túːm]

We found this comb on his tomb.

このくしが彼の墓の上にありました。

- □ comb ［名］くし
- □ tomb ［名］墓

track 33 絵を見ながら **Listen to the English!**
発音やつづりが似た単語を、まとめて体で覚えよう！

解説は次ページ

129	sledge　edge
130	bump　bumper
131	aunt　jaunt
132	grain　grin

Day 4

129 sledge [slédʒ] | edge [édʒ]

We were lucky that our **sledge** stopped at the **edge** of the glacier.

僕たちのそりが氷河の端で止まったのは運がよかった。

- □ sledge［名］そり
- □ edge［名］端、ふち
- □ glacier［名］氷河

130 bump [bʌ́mp] | bumper [bʌ́mpər]

The two vehicles **bumped** into each other, completely destroying their front **bumpers**.

2台の車両は衝突して、前のバンパーが大破した。

- □ vehicle［名］車、車両
- □ bump［動］ぶつかる、衝突する
- □ destroy［動］〜を破壊する
- □ bumper［名］バンパー、緩衝装置

131 aunt [ǽnt | ɑ́ːnt] | jaunt [dʒɔ́ːnt]

I must accompany my **aunt** for a **jaunt** into the city this afternoon.

今日の午後は、おばさんに付き添って街に行かなくちゃならないんだ。

- □ accompany［動］〜に同行する、付き添う
- □ aunt［名］おば
- □ jaunt［名］散策、小旅行

132 grain [gréin] | grin [grín]

"There isn't a **grain** of truth in what he's saying," she said with a **grin**.

「彼の言っていることは嘘八百よ」と、彼女はにやにやしながら言った。

- □ grain［名］穀粒、穀物 / □ a grain of ほんのわずかの〜
- □ truth［名］事実
- □ grin［名］（歯を見せて）にこりと笑うこと

| track 34 | 絵を見ながら **Listen to the English!** 発音やつづりが似た単語を、まとめて体で覚えよう！ | 解説は次ページ |

133 grin　grid

134 grid　grind

135 conscious　conscience

136 boaster　boast　booster

133 grin [grín] | grid [gríd]

The athlete grinned as he strode up to the starting grid.

その選手は大股で歩きながら、にやにやしてスタート位置についた。

- □ athlete［名］運動選手
- □ stride［動］大股で歩く
- □ grin［動］（歯を見せて）にこりと笑う
- □ starting grid　スタート位置

134 grid [gríd] | grind [gráind]

Don't ask me to clean the grid while I'm still grinding the coffee beans.

ぼくがコーヒー豆をひいている間は、格子を掃除しろって言わないでくれ。

- □ grid［名］（窓などの）格子
- □ grind［動］〜をすりつぶす、ひく

135 conscious [kánʃəs | kɔ́n-] | conscience [kánʃəns | kɔ́n-]

He's a money-conscious person without any conscience.

彼は良心を持ち合わせていない、拝金主義者だ。

- □ conscious［形］意識した、重視した / □ money-conscious　金銭に対する執着が強い
- □ conscience［名］良心、道徳心

136 boaster [bóustər] | boast [bóust] | booster [búːstər]

He's nothing but a boaster if he boasts that he can send a spaceship into orbit without boosters.

彼がブースターなしで宇宙船を軌道に乗せられると自慢しているなら、ただのほらふきだ。

- □ boaster［名］自慢する人
- □ orbit［名］軌道
- □ boast［動］自慢する
- □ booster［名］補助推進ロケット

絵を見ながら Listen to the English!
発音やつづりが似た単語を、まとめて体で覚えよう！

解説は次ページ

137 advertise adverse

138 chop chopper

139 explicit implicit

Absolutely not!
WTO

140 fun funky

advertise, adverse / chop, chopper / explicit, implicit / fun, funky

137 advertise [ǽdvərtàiz] | adverse [ædvə́ːrs]

We need to advertise to find someone who can solve our problems before these adverse decisions drag us under.

この不利な決断がわれわれを窮地に陥れる前に、問題を解決できる人員を募集すべきだ。

- □ advertise［動］（求人）広告を出す　□ adverse［形］不都合な

138 chop [tʃɑ́p] | chopper [tʃɑ́pər]

They had to chop out a space for the chopper to land.

木を切ってヘリコプターが着陸するためのスペースを作る必要があった。

- □ chop［動］たたき切る / □ chop out a space for （木を）切って〜のためのスペースを作る
- □ chopper［名］ヘリコプター、切る人
- □ land［動］（飛行機が）着陸する

139 explicit [iksplísit] | implicit [implísit]

I've been given explicit instructions not to be affected by any implicit threats in this negotiation.

私はこの交渉で暗黙の脅しにひるむなという明確な指示を受けている。

- □ explicit［形］明確な　　　　　□ instruction［名］指示、命令
- □ affect［動］〜に影響を及ぼす　□ implicit［形］暗黙の
- □ threat［名］脅し　　　　　　　□ negotiation［名］交渉

140 fun [fʌ́n] | funky [fʌ́ŋki]

It's good fun to play funky music.

ファンキーな音楽を演奏するのは楽しいよ。

- □ fun［名］楽しみ
- □ funky［形］ファンキーな、いかす / □ funky music 黒人的なブルースやゴスペルの影響を受けた音楽

92

絵を見ながら Listen to the English!
発音やつづりが似た単語を、まとめて体で覚えよう！

track 36　解説は次ページ

141 clue　glue

142 restrict　district

143 emit　remit

144 fuse　refuse　defuse

clue, glue / restrict, district / emit, remit / fuse, refuse, defuse

141 clue [klúː] | glue [glúː]

I don't have a clue how they make this super glue.

どうやってその強力な接着剤を作るのか、皆目見当がつかない。

- □ clue［名］（問題を解く）手がかり、ヒント
- □ glue［名］接着剤、のり

142 restrict [ristríkt] | district [dístrikt]

The sale of alcohol is restricted in this district.

この地方ではアルコールの販売は規制されていますよ。

- □ restrict［動］〜を規制する、制限する
- □ district［名］地域、地方

143 emit [imít] | remit [rimít]

He emitted a few curses when he remitted payment to his divorced wife.

彼は離婚した妻に金を送るときに、ののしりの言葉を発した。

- □ emit［動］（声などを）発する
- □ remit［動］（金を）送る
- □ curse［名］ののしり
- □ divorced［形］離婚した

144 fuse [fjúːz] | refuse [rifjúːz] | defuse [di(ː)fjúːz]

When he saw that the time bomb had three fuses he simply refused to defuse it.

彼は時限爆弾に信管が3つ付いているのを見て、それを外すのを嫌だと拒んだ。

- □ fuse［名］（爆弾などの）信管
- □ refuse［動］〜を拒否する
- □ defuse［動］（爆弾などから）信管を取り除く、安全にする（*defuse* a dangerous situation 危険な状況を打開する）

Day 5

Keywords for Day 5

- **track 37**: are, ware / bank, lanky / efficient, deficient / belly, bell
- **track 38**: definitely, indefinitely / deform, reform / inflate, deflate, reflate / accredit, credit
- **track 39**: humble, fumble / hot, lot, rot, rote / competition, repetition / sue, issue
- **track 40**: compact, impact / bag, beg, fag / buckle, buck / cram, cramp
- **track 41**: affluent, fluent / conflict, afflict / confirm, affirm / affect, effect
- **track 42**: float, afloat / brook, crook / jangle, jungle / investigate, instigate
- **track 43**: hepatitis, appetite / dizzy, dazzling / curb, curl / decent, decant
- **track 44**: grumble, crumble, crumb / horrible, hobble / frank, flank / colleague, league
- **track 45**: boom, boon / luck, lurk / scam, can, scan / infect, effect

track 37 絵を見ながら **Listen to the English!**
発音やつづりが似た単語を、まとめて体で覚えよう！

解説は次ページ

145 are　ware

146 bank　lanky

147 efficient　deficient

148 belly　bell

are, ware / bank, lanky / efficient, deficient / belly, bell

145 **are**[áːr] | **ware**[wéər]

Watch out! You are going to be hit by your own wares.
気をつけろ！　自分の商品に当たるぞ。

- □ Watch out!　危ない！　気をつけて！
- □ are［動］be の二人称単数および、各人称複数の現在形
- □ hit［動］〜にぶつかる
- □ ware［名］商品、売品（通例 one's wares）

146 **bank**[bǽŋk] | **lanky**[lǽŋki]

The bank manager was a young, lanky man.
銀行の支配人はひょろっとした若い男だった。

- □ bank［名］銀行
- □ manager［名］支配人、経営者
- □ lanky［形］ひょろっとした、やせこけた

147 **efficient**[ifíʃənt] | **deficient**[difíʃənt]

This machine is very efficient, but the supply of raw material needed to run it is deficient.
この機械はとても有能だけど、それを動かす原料の供給が不足している。

- □ efficient［形］効力のある
- □ raw material　原料
- □ deficient［形］不足した
- □ supply［名］供給
- □ run［動］（機械を）動かす

148 **belly**[béli] | **bell**[bél]

As he had been snacking, he already had a full belly when he heard the dinner bell.
彼は軽食をとっていたので、食事を知らせる鐘がなったときにはすでに満腹だった。

- □ belly［名］腹 / □ have a full belly　満腹だ / □ have an empty belly　空腹だ
- □ bell［名］鐘 / □ a dinner bell　食事を知らせる鐘

絵を見ながら Listen to the English!

発音やつづりが似た単語を、まとめて体で覚えよう！

解説は次ページ

149 definitely　indefinitely

150 deform　reform

151 inflate　deflate　reflate

152 accredit　credit

definitely, indefinitely / deform, reform / inflate, deflate, reflate / accredit, credit

149 definitely [défənitli] | indefinitely [indéfənitli]

The refugees should definitely be allowed to stay here indefinitely.

間違いなく、難民たちはここに永住することを認められるべきだ。

- □ refugee［名］避難者、難民
- □ definitely［副］間違いなく、確かに
- □ indefinitely［副］無期限に（postpone *indefinitely* 無期延期する）

150 deform [difɔ́ːrm] | reform [rifɔ́ːrm]

The president's face was deformed with anger when I told him about my ideas for company reform.

社内改革についての私の考えを伝えたとき、社長の顔は怒りでゆがんだ。

- □ deform［動］〜を変形させる、ゆがめる（Heat *deforms* plastic. 熱はプラスチックを変形させる）
- □ reform［名］改革、改善

151 inflate [infléit] | deflate [difléit] | reflate [rifléit]

It is the government's game to first inflate the currency, then deflate it, only to reflate it again later.

通貨をつり上げ、次に収縮させるのは、後で再膨張させるための政府のゲームだ。

- □ inflate［動］（物価を）つり上げる
- □ deflate［動］（通貨を）収縮させる
- □ currency［名］通貨、貨幣
- □ reflate［動］（通貨を）再膨張させる

152 accredit [əkrédit] | credit [krédit]

Our school is internationally accredited, so our students' credits are accepted abroad.

わが校は国際的に正式認可されているので、生徒の履修単位は海外でも有効だ。

- □ accredit［動］〜を認可する / □ accredited［形］認可された
- □ credit［名］履修単位
- □ accepted［形］一般に認められた

絵を見ながら Listen to the English!

発音やつづりが似た単語を、まとめて体で覚えよう！

解説は次ページ

153 humble fumble

154 hot lot rot rote

155 competition repetition

156 sue issue

humble, fumble / hot, lot, rot, rote / competition, repetition / sue, issue

153 humble [hʌ́mbəl] | fumble [fʌ́mbəl]

The salesman was humbled as he fumbled about his briefcase for a pen.

営業マンはかばんの中のペンをもたもたと手探りしながら、みじめな気分になった。

- □ humble［動］（人を）屈辱的な状態にする
- □ fumble［動］（不器用に）手探りする
- □ briefcase［名］ブリーフケース、書類かばん

154 hot [hát] | lot [lát] | rot [rát] | rote [róut]

Learning English is hot now, but it's a lot of rot if you're told you can learn it by rote.

今、英語学習が人気だけど、丸暗記で覚えられるなどと言うのは、まったくくだらない。

- □ hot［形］人気のある　　□ lot［名］たくさん
- □ rot［名］くだらないもの
- □ rote［名］機械的な暗記 / □ learn ... by rote　…を丸暗記する

155 competition [kàmpətíʃən] | repetition [rèpətíʃən]

This crossword competition is a repetition of the one we had a few weeks ago.

このクロスワード大会は数週間前にやったやつのまったくの繰り返しだよ。

- □ crossword［名］クロスワードパズル
- □ competition［名］競争、競技会、コンペ
- □ repetition［名］繰り返し

156 sue [súː] | issue [íʃuː]

The parents are threatening to sue if the issue of free milk to schoolchildren is discontinued.

親たちは、学童への無料ミルクの配給が廃止されるなら、訴えるつもりだと脅している。

- □ threaten［動］〜と脅す　　□ sue［動］告訴する
- □ issue［名］配給、支給　　□ discontinue［動］〜をやめる

絵を見ながら Listen to the English!
発音やつづりが似た単語を、まとめて体で覚えよう！

解説は次ページ

157 compact impact

158 bag beg fag

159 buckle buck

160 cram cramp

compact, impact / bag, beg, fag / buckle, buck / cram, cramp

[157] **compact**[kəmpǽkt | kám-] | **impact**[ímpækt]

Such a compact computer is bound to have a great impact on the computer market.

これほど小型のコンピュータなら、市場に大きな影響をもたらすだろう。

- □ compact［形］小さくて携帯しやすい
- □ be bound to　きっと～する
- □ impact［名］影響、衝撃

[158] **bag**[bǽg] | **beg**[bég] | **fag**[fǽg]

I was talking to that lady with the bag only because she tried to beg a fag from me.

あのかばんを持った婦人が僕にタバコをくれと言ったからしゃべっていただけだよ。

- □ bag［名］かばん、バッグ
- □ beg［動］（人に）～を乞う、ねだる
- □ fag［名］巻きタバコ

[159] **buckle**[bʌ́kəl] | **buck**[bʌ́k]

Buckle up, or we'll be fined a hundred bucks.

シートベルトを締めろよ、でないと100ドルの罰金を取られるぜ。

- □ buckle up　シートベルトを締める
- □ fine［動］～に罰金を科する
- □ buck［名］ドル、金

[160] **cram**[krǽm] | **cramp**[krǽmp]

I don't see how you can cram any more people into that already cramped house.

あんなに窮屈な家に、これ以上どうやったって人は詰め込めないだろう。

- □ see［動］～が分かる
- □ cram［動］～を詰め込む、押し込む
- □ cramped［形］狭苦しい、窮屈な

track 41 絵を見ながら **Listen to the English!**
発音やつづりが似た単語を、まとめて体で覚えよう！

解説は次ページ

161 affluent　fluent

162 conflict　afflict

163 confirm　affirm

164 affect　effect

105

affluent, fluent / conflict, afflict / confirm, affirm / affect, effect

161 affluent [ǽfluənt] | fluent [flúːənt]

She's from an affluent family and can speak fluent French.

彼女は裕福な家の出で、フランス語がペラペラなんだ。

- □ affluent［形］豊かな、裕福な
- □ fluent［形］流暢な
- □ French［名］フランス語

162 conflict [kánflikt] | afflict [əflíkt]

Armed conflicts afflict everyone, especially defenseless men, women and children.

武力衝突は、武器を持たない男女や子供をはじめとするすべての人々を苦しめる。

- □ armed［形］武装した
- □ afflict［動］〜を苦しめる、悩ます
- □ conflict［名］闘争、衝突
- □ defenseless［形］武器を持たない

163 confirm [kənfə́ːrm] | affirm [əfə́ːrm]

In order to confim her feelings for you, go and affirm your love for her.

彼女の気持ちを確認するために、おまえの彼女への愛を誓ってこいよ。

- □ confirm［動］〜を確認する、立証する
- □ affirm［動］〜を断言する、主張する

164 affect [əfékt] | effect [ifékt]

Smoking does affect your health, with the direct effect being that you damage your healthy lungs.

喫煙は健康に影響します。直接的な危険性としては、健康な肺を損なうことが挙げられます。

- □ affect［動］〜に影響する
- □ healthy［形］健康な、健康に役立つ
- □ effect［名］効果、結果
- □ lung［名］肺

絵を見ながら Listen to the English!
発音やつづりが似た単語を、まとめて体で覚えよう！

track 42

解説は次ページ

165 float　afloat

166 brook　crook

167 jangle　jungle

168 investigate　instigate

float, afloat / brook, crook / jangle, jungle / investigate, instigate

165 float [flóut] | afloat [əflóut]

He floated in the life raft for days, bailing it out to keep it afloat.

彼は何日も救命ボートで漂った。沈まないように水をかき出しながら。

- □ float［動］漂う、流れる
- □ bail out （船から水を）かき出す
- □ life raft　救命いかだ、ゴムボート
- □ afloat［副］浮かんで、漂って

166 brook [brúk] | crook [krúk]

He would never brook having a crook in the family.

家族に泥棒がいるなんてことを、彼は絶対に許さないだろう。

- □ brook［動］〜を我慢する、忍ぶ
- □ crook［名］曲がったもの、泥棒、悪党

167 jangle [dʒǽŋgəl] | jungle [dʒʌ́ŋgl]

We thought we heard horse bells jangling in the jungle.

ジャングルで馬の鈴がジャラジャラと鳴っているのが聞こえた気がした。

- □ jangle［動］ジャンジャン鳴る（The brass bells *jangled* on the horse's collar. 真ちゅうのベルが馬の首元でうるさく鳴った）
- □ jungle［名］熱帯の密林、ジャングル

168 investigate [invéstəgèit] | instigate [ínstəgèit]

The police investigated to see who instigated the incident.

警察は、誰がこの事件を扇動したかを捜査した。

- □ investigate［動］〜を調査する、捜査する
- □ instigate［動］〜を扇動する、主導する
- □ incident［名］事件

絵を見ながら Listen to the English!

発音やつづりが似た単語を、まとめて体で覚えよう！

track 43

解説は次ページ

169 hepatitis　appetite

170 dizzy　dazzling

171 curb　curl

172 decent　decant

Day 5

109

hepatitis, appetite / dizzy, dazzling / curb, curl / decent, decant

169 hepatitis [hèpətáitis] | appetite [ǽpətàit]

When you get hepatitis, you lose your appetite for oily food.

肝炎になると、油っこいものが食べたくなくなる。

- □ hepatitis [名] 肝炎
- □ appetite [名] 食欲
- □ oily [形] 油っこい

170 dizzy [dízi] | dazzling [dǽzliŋ]

I got dizzy just watching his dazzling performance.

彼の見事な演技を見ているだけで目が回った。

- □ dizzy [形] 目が回る、くらくらする
- □ dazzling [形] 見事な

171 curb [kə́ːrb] | curl [kə́ːrl]

The doctor said that, if I didn't want to lose my hair, I needed to curb my desire to curl my hair every day.

医者は私に、髪を残したいなら毎日髪の毛をカールしたいという欲求を抑えなければならないと言った。

- □ curb [動] 〜を抑制する、抑える
- □ desire [名] 欲望、願望
- □ curl [動] （髪を）カールさせる、巻き毛にする

172 decent [díːsənt] | decant [dikǽnt]

A decent wine may need to be decanted several times.

上質のワインは、何度か容器を移し替える必要があるかもしれない。

- □ decent [形] かなりの、まずまずの、上品な
- □ decant [動] （ワインなどを）他の容器に静かに移す

絵を見ながら Listen to the English!
発音やつづりが似た単語を、まとめて体で覚えよう！

173 grumble crumble crumb

174 horrible hobble

175 frank flank

176 colleague league

grumble, crumble, crumb / horrible, hobble / frank, flank / colleague, league

173 grumble[grʌ́mbəl] | crumble[krʌ́mbl] | crumb[krʌ́m]

Mom always grumbles when I crumble my bread and drop the crumbs on the floor.

僕がくだいたパンのくずを床に落とすと、ママはいつもぶつぶつ言う。

- □ grumble［動］不平を言う、ぶつぶつ言う
- □ crumble［動］〜を粉々にする、砕く
- □ crumb［名］（パンなどの）かけら、くず

174 horrible[hɔ́(ː)rəbl | hɑ́r-] | hobble[hɑ́bəl]

It's horrible to have to hobble along with my legs hurting like this.

こんなふうに痛む足を引きずって歩かなくちゃいけないのは最悪だ。

- □ horrible［形］最悪な、悲惨な
- □ hobble［動］足を引きずって歩く
- □ hurt［動］痛みを感じる

175 frank[frǽŋk] | flank[flǽŋk]

To be frank, we will be defeated if the enemy attacks us on our left flank.

率直に言って、敵が左の側面から攻撃してきたら、われわれは負けます。

- □ frank［形］率直な / □ to be frank　率直に言って
- □ be defeated　敗北する
- □ flank［名］側面

176 colleague[kɑ́liːg] | league[líːg]

She is my colleague and a member of the Youth League.

彼女は僕の同僚で、青年リーグのメンバーなんだ。

- □ colleague［名］同僚
- □ youth［名］青年、若者
- □ league［名］同盟

track 45 絵を見ながら Listen to the English!

発音やつづりが似た単語を、まとめて体で覚えよう！

解説は次ページ

177 boom　boon

178 luck　lurk

179 scam　can　scan

180 infect　effect

177 boom [búːm] | boon [búːn]

The post-war baby boom was a great boon to the economy.

戦後のベビーブームは、経済にとって大きな恩恵だった。

- baby boom　ベビーブーム
- boon［名］恩恵（The radio is a great *boon* to the blind. ラジオは目の不自由な人にとって、とても有り難いものだ）

178 luck [lʌ́k] | lurk [lə́ːrk]

He had great luck photographing the tiger lurking under the tree he was in.

自分のいる木の下に隠れていたトラを撮影できて、彼は幸運だった。

- luck［名］運、幸運
- lurk［動］潜む、隠れる（doubts that *lurk* in my mind 私の心に潜む疑い）

179 scam [skǽm] | can [kǽn] | scan [skǽn]

What a scam! No one can scan people's brains with their bare eyes.

それは詐欺だよ！　人間の脳は裸眼では見られないんだから。

- scam［名］ペテン、詐欺
- can［助動］〜できる
- scan［動］〜をざっと見る、画像を取り込む
- bare［形］裸の / *bare* eyes　裸眼

180 infect [infékt] | effect [ifékt]

Don't infect me with your cold! I don't want to suffer from its horrible effects.

あなたの風邪をうつさないでよ！　つらい症状に苦しみたくないんだから。

- infect［動］〜に（病気を）うつす、感染させる
- suffer［動］病気をする、苦しむ
- effect［名］結果、影響

Day 6

Keywords for Day 6

- **track 46** coy, decoy / resolutely, absolutely / booty, boot / detractor, contractor

- **track 47** definite, infinite / crow, crowd / honk, horn / curb, curd

- **track 48** fringe, infringe / it, tit, tat / foggy, fogy / attempt, tempt

- **track 49** reject, inject / kid, skid / elaborate, collaborate / nag, nab, bag

- **track 50** goal, goad / assess, access / access, excess / hatter, shatter

- **track 51** depreciate, appreciate / gape, gap / indicate, dictate / duck, chuck

- **track 52** lick, slick / lucky, yucky / expression, impression / gal, pal

- **track 53** angle, tangle / gum, glum / bore, gore / posture, gesture

- **track 54** bad, bald / duplex, triplex, complex / attention, retention / tug, hug, mug

絵を見ながら Listen to the English!

発音やつづりが似た単語を、まとめて体で覚えよう！

解説は次ページ

181 coy　decoy

182 resolutely　absolutely

183 booty　boot

184 detractor　contractor

coy, decoy / resolutely, absolutely / booty, boot / detractor, contractor

181 coy [kɔ́i] | decoy [díːkɔi]

I'm afraid her coy smile was only a decoy to make you believe her sad story.

彼女の純情そうな笑顔は、悲しい身の上話を君に信じさせるための罠だったんだよ。

- □ coy ［形］ はにかんだ、恥ずかしそうな、純情ぶった
- □ decoy ［名］ おとり、おとり用の鳥の模型

182 resolutely [rézəlùːtli] | absolutely [ǽbsəlùːtli]

The king resolutely declared that he was absolutely right.

王様は自分が絶対的に正しいと断言した。

- □ resolutely ［副］ 決然と、断固として
- □ declare ［動］ 〜を明言する
- □ absolutely ［副］ 絶対に、まったく

183 booty [búːti] | boot [búːt]

Do you think you'll get more booty by licking my boots?

僕にへつらえばもっと物が手に入ると思ってるのか？

- □ booty ［名］ 戦利品、獲物
- □ lick a person's boots （人に）こびへつらう

184 detractor [ditrǽktər] | contractor [kəntrǽktər]

He's just a detractor; everybody knows that I legally employed all my contractors.

彼はただ誹謗しているだけだ。私が法にのっとって請け負い業者を雇ったことは誰でも知っている。

- □ detractor ［名］ 中傷する人
- □ employ ［動］ （人を）雇う
- □ legally ［副］ 合法的に
- □ contractor ［名］ 請け負い業者

絵を見ながら Listen to the English!

発音やつづりが似た単語を、まとめて体で覚えよう！

解説は次ページ

185 definite　infinite

186 crow　crowd

187 honk　horn

188 curb　curd

119

definite, infinite / crow, crowd / honk, horn / curb, curd

185 **definite** [défənit] | **infinite** [ínfənət]

Whatever questions your children ask, do your best to give them as definite answers as possible, with infinite patience.

子どもが何を聞いても、なるべく忍耐力をもってはっきり答えるよう最大限努力してください。

☐ definite ［形］明確な　　　　　☐ infinite ［形］無期限の、寛大な

186 **crow** [króu] | **crowd** [kráud]

In the old days, crows used to crowd onto the power cables and crow with pleasure.

昔は、カラスが電線に群がって楽しそうに鳴いていたものだ。

☐ crow ［名］カラス　［動］鳴く
☐ crowd ［動］群がる、押し寄せる
☐ pleasure ［名］喜び、楽しさ

187 **honk** [hὰŋk | hɔ́ŋk] | **horn** [hɔ́ːrn]

Just honk your horn if she doesn't come out soon.

彼女がすぐ出てこなかったら、警笛を鳴らせばいいよ。

☐ honk ［動］（クラクションを）鳴らす
☐ horn ［名］警笛、クラクション

188 **curb** [kə́ːrb] | **curd** [kə́ːrd]

Trying hard to curb her jealousy, she kept on eating the bean curd.

彼女は嫉妬心を何とか抑えようと、豆腐を食べ続けた。

☐ curb ［動］（感情を）抑える、抑制する
☐ bean curd　豆腐

track 48 絵を見ながら **Listen to the English!**
発音やつづりが似た単語を、まとめて体で覚えよう！

解説は次ページ

189	fringe infringe
190	it tit tat
191	foggy fogy
192	attempt tempt

Day 1
Day 2
Day 3
Day 4
Day 5
Day 6
Day 7
Day 8
Day 9
Day 10

189 fringe [frínd ʒ] | infringe [infrínd ʒ]

Free healthcare is one of our fringe benefits and if you cancel it, you will infringe upon the law.

無料の健康管理は私たちの給与外特典のひとつです。取り消せば法に触れますよ。

- □ healthcare［名］健康管理
- □ fringe benefit　給与外の諸手当
- □ infringe［動］（法律などを）侵害する

190 it [ít] | tit [tít] | tat [tǽt]

It was just tit for tat.

売り言葉に買い言葉だった。

- □ it［代］それ
- □ tit for tat　しっぺ返し、仕返し、売り言葉に買い言葉

191 foggy [fɔ́(ː)gi] | fogy [fóugi]

I haven't the foggiest idea what that old fogy was going on about that foggy morning.

あの霧深い朝、あの時代遅れの頑固者が何をまくしたてていたのか、見当もつかない。

- □ foggy［形］霧の深い、ぼんやりした / □ haven't the foggiest idea　見当もつかない
- □ fogy［名］時代遅れの頑固者

192 attempt [ətémpt] | tempt [témpt]

I once attempted to tempt her with a large salary, but that backfired.

以前、彼女を高い給料で誘惑しようとして裏目に出たよ。

- □ attempt［動］〜を試みる、企てる　　□ tempt［動］〜を誘惑する
- □ salary［名］給料　　　　　　　　　　□ backfire［動］〜が裏目に出る

絵を見ながら **Listen to the English!**
発音やつづりが似た単語を、まとめて体で覚えよう！

解説は次ページ

193 reject　inject

194 kid　skid

195 elaborate　collaborate

196 nag　nab　bag

reject, inject / kid, skid / elaborate, collaborate / nag, nab, bag

[193] **reject**[ridʒékt] | **inject**[indʒékt]

He rejected having an operation and instead asked his doctor to inject him with the new drug.

彼は手術を拒否し、その代わりに新薬を注射してくれるよう医師に頼んだ。

□ reject［動］〜を拒絶する、拒否する
□ operation［名］手術、事業
□ inject［動］〜に注射する、注入する

[194] **kid**[kíd] | **skid**[skíd]

You should have reminded your kid that he might skid on the ice.

お子さんに氷の上は滑りやすいことを注意しておくべきでした。

□ remind ... that　…に〜であることを思い出させる
□ kid［名］子ども
□ skid［動］滑る

[195] **elaborate**[ilǽbərət] | **collaborate**[kəlǽbərèit]

The officer made up an elaborate excuse to deny that he was collaborating with the enemy.

警官は敵に協力していることを否定するために、念入りな言い訳を考え出した。

□ elaborate［形］念入りな、精密な
□ deny［動］〜を否定する
□ collaborate with　（敵側に）協力する、（人と）共同で行う

[196] **nag**[nǽg] | **nab**[nǽb] | **bag**[bǽg]

She nagged at the policman for his failure to nab the lad who had snatched her bag.

彼女は警官が彼女のかばんをひったくった少年を捕まえられなかったことに対してうるさく言った。

□ nag at　〜に口うるさく言う　　□ nab［動］〜を取り押さえる
□ lad［名］少年、若者　　　　　 □ snatch［動］〜をひったくる
□ bag［名］かばん、バッグ

track 50 絵を見ながら **Listen to the English!**
発音やつづりが似た単語を、まとめて体で覚えよう！

解説は次ページ

197 goal　goad

198 assess　access

199 access　excess

200 hatter　shatter

[197] **goal** [góul] | **goad** [góud]

Since going to college is not his goal, it's no use goading him to improve his grades.

彼の目標は大学に入ることではないから、成績を上げるようせっついてもむだよ。

☐ goal［名］目標
☐ goad［動］〜を駆り立てる、刺激する
☐ grade［名］成績

[198] **assess** [əsés] | **access** [ǽkses]

The government will assess the possibility of allowing public access to the central database.

政府は中央のデータベースに一般市民もアクセスができるようにする可能性について、判断を下す。

☐ assess［動］〜を評価する、査定する
☐ public access　公共のアクセス
☐ central database　中央のデータベース

[199] **access** [ǽkses] | **excess** [iksés]

You may access the Internet but do not use it to excess.

インターネットを使ってもいいけど、やり過ぎはダメよ。

☐ access［動］〜にアクセスする、接近する
☐ excess［名］過度、過剰 / ☐ to excess　過度に

[200] **hatter** [hǽtər] | **shatter** [ʃǽtər]

He was as mad as a hatter when his hopes were shattered.

彼はすべての望みが断たれ、完全にキレてしまった。

☐ mad as a hatter　頭がすっかり狂って、完全に頭にきて
☐ shatter［動］〜を打ち砕く、粉砕する（A stone *shattered* my window. 石がうちの窓を割った）

絵を見ながら Listen to the English!

track 51　解説は次ページ

発音やつづりが似た単語を、まとめて体で覚えよう！

201 depreciate　appreciate

Thank you anyway!

202 gape　gap

203 indicate　dictate

204 duck　chuck

201 depreciate [dipríːʃieit] | appreciate [əpríːʃieit]

Though the shares eventually depreciated in value, I do appreciate the advice you gave me on that matter.
結局株は下がってしまったけど、その件についてのアドバイスには感謝します。

- □ share［名］株、株式
- □ depreciate［動］価値が下がる
- □ appreciate［動］〜を感謝する、高く評価する

202 gape [géip] | gap [gǽp]

She gaped at the dog through the big gap in the fence.
彼女は塀の大きな割れ目の向こうの犬をぼうぜんと見た。

- □ gape［動］口をぽかんとあけて見る
- □ gap［名］割れ目、穴
- □ fence［名］塀、さく

203 indicate [índikèit] | dictate [díkteit]

Research indicates that men can no longer dictate to women what they should do.
調査は、もはや男性が女性がすべきことについて指図できないことを示している。

- □ research［名］研究、調査
- □ indicate［動］〜を指し示す
- □ dictate［動］〜を命令する

204 duck [dʌ́k] | chuck [tʃʌ́k]

I quickly ducked when he chucked the ball at me.
彼が球を投げたとき、僕は素早く頭を下げた。

- □ quickly［副］速く、敏速に
- □ duck［動］ひょいとかがむ、ひょいと頭を下げる
- □ chuck［動］〜をほうる、軽く投げる

絵を見ながら Listen to the English!
発音やつづりが似た単語を、まとめて体で覚えよう！

track 52

解説は次ページ

205 lick slick

206 lucky yucky

207 expression impression

208 gal pal

lick, slick / lucky, yucky / expression, impression / gal, pal

205 **lick** [lík] | **slick** [slík]

It's dangerous to lick your ice cream cone on this slick road.

このすべりやすい道でアイスクリームをなめるのは危ないよ。

□ lick［動］〜をなめる
□ slick［形］つるつるした、なめらかな

206 **lucky** [lʌ́ki] | **yucky** [jʌ́ki]

You're lucky that your dad doesn't force you to eat yucky veggies every day.

毎日お父さんにまずい野菜を無理に食べさせられなくて、あなたは幸運よ。

□ lucky［形］幸運な、運のいい
□ force ... to do　…に無理に〜させる
□ yucky［形］まずい、気持ち悪い　　□ veggy［名］野菜

207 **expression** [ikspréʃən] | **impression** [impréʃən]

Her horrified expression left a deep impression on him.

彼女の恐怖の表情が彼に強い印象を残した。

□ horrified［形］恐怖に襲われた、ショックを受けた
□ expression［名］表情、表現
□ impression［名］印象、感動

208 **gal** [gǽl] | **pal** [pǽl]

This gal is my pal.

この娘は僕の友達なんだ。

□ gal［名］女の子、少女
□ pal［名］仲間、友達

track 53 絵を見ながら Listen to the English!

発音やつづりが似た単語を、まとめて体で覚えよう！

解説は次ページ

209 angle　tangle

210 gum　glum

211 bore　gore

212 posture　gesture

angle, tangle / gum, glum / bore, gore / posture, gesture

209 angle [ǽŋgl] | tangle [tǽŋgl]

From the angle of being good for you, seaweed is ideal, though it does tangle easily when you wash it.

海草は健康食の観点からは理想的だが、洗うときにからまりやすい。

□ angle［名］観点、角度 / □ from the angle of 〜の観点から
□ ideal［形］理想的な
□ tangle［動］もつれる、からまる

210 gum [gʌ́m] | glum [glʌ́m]

He was up a gum tree and feeling very glum indeed.

彼は窮地に陥り、すごく落ち込んでいた。

□ gum tree　ゴムの木 / □ be up a gum tree　窮地に陥って、追い詰められて
□ glum［形］陰気な、落胆した
□ indeed［副］本当に

211 bore [bɔ́ːr] | gore [gɔ́ːr]

What's boring about a bull almost goring a matador?

雄牛がもう少しで闘牛士を突き刺そうとしているところの何が退屈なんだ？

□ bore［動］（人を）退屈させる / □ boring［形］退屈な
□ bull［名］雄牛
□ gore［動］〜を突く、突き刺す
□ matador［名］主役の闘牛士（マタドール）

212 posture [pʌ́stʃər] | gesture [dʒéstʃər]

The secretary changed her posture, shrugging her shoulders in a gesture of impatience.

秘書は姿勢を変えて、我慢できないというように肩をすくめた。

□ posture［名］姿勢、態度　　　□ shrug［動］（肩を）すくめる
□ gesture［名］身ぶり、しぐさ　　□ impatience［名］短気、切望

track 54 絵を見ながら **Listen to the English!**
発音やつづりが似た単語を、まとめて体で覚えよう！

解説は次ページ

213 bad　bald

214 duplex　triplex　complex

215 attention　retention

216 tug　hug　mug

bad, bald / duplex, triplex, complex / attention, retention / tug, hug, mug

213 bad [bǽd] | bald [bɔ́ːld]

The bad news is that all the tires on our car are bald and need to be changed.

悪い知らせだよ。うちの車のタイヤは全部つるつるにすり減っていて、交換しなきゃならない。

☐ bad ［形］悪い、よくない
☐ bald ［形］はげた、（タイヤが）すり減った (He's going bald. 彼はハゲかけている)

214 duplex [djúːpleks] | triplex [trípleks] | complex [kəmpléks]

To build a duplex or a triplex is not that complex.

2階建てアパートを作るのも3階建てアパートを作るのも、それほど複雑なことではありませんよ。

☐ duplex ［名］複層式アパート、2世帯住宅
☐ triplex ［名］3階建てアパート
☐ complex ［形］入り組んだ、複雑な

215 attention [əténʃən] | retention [riténʃən]

You need to pay attention to this patient's urinary retention.

患者の尿の貯留に注意する必要があります。

☐ attention ［名］注意 / ☐ pay attention to ～に注意を払う
☐ urinary ［形］尿の
☐ retention ［名］保持、維持

216 tug [tʌ́g] | hug [hʌ́g] | mug [mʌ́g]

After the tug boat rescued him, we hugged and celebrated with a mug of coffee.

タグボートが彼を救助した後、われわれは抱き合ってコーヒーで乾杯した。

☐ tug ［名］強く引くこと / ☐ tug boat えい航船、タグボート
☐ hug ［動］抱擁する
☐ mug ［名］マグカップ、ジョッキ

Day 7

Keywords for Day 7

- **track 55** — lucky, mucky / dad, dab / date, sedate / fuss, fuse
- **track 56** — ensure, leisure / err, error / rarely, barely / division, vision
- **track 57** — heel, reel / impulsion, compulsion / institution, constitution / insolent, insolvent
- **track 58** — replete, complete / hell, hello / wedge, edge / case, chaste, chase
- **track 59** — lubricate, lubricant / criteria, bacteria / friction, fraction / installation, distillation
- **track 60** — fumble, tumble / dove, love, glove / moan, loan / create, cream
- **track 61** — lump, hump / evaluate, evacuate / appreciate, appropriate / interest, disinterest
- **track 62** — deserve, conserve / invest, divest / kidney, kid / bash, dash, cash
- **track 63** — creed, breed / jail, bail / contention, intention / include, exclude

track 55 絵を見ながら **Listen to the English!**
発音やつづりが似た単語を、まとめて体で覚えよう！

解説は次ページ

217 lucky　mucky

218 dad　dab

219 date　sedate

220 fuss　fuse

lucky, mucky / dad, dab / date, sedate / fuss, fuse

217 lucky [lʌ́ki] | mucky [mʌ́ki]

You're lucky that you don't have to go out on such a mucky day.

こんな蒸し暑い日に出かけずにすんで、君はついているよ。

☐ lucky［形］運のいい
☐ mucky［形］じめじめした、蒸し暑い

218 dad [dǽd] | dab [dǽb]

Her dad dabbed some cream on her face.

父親が彼女の顔にクリームを軽く塗った。

☐ dad［名］お父さん
☐ dab［動］〜を軽く塗る、軽くたたく

219 sedate [sidéit] | date [déit]

Our sedate old neighbor gave us a bag of dates for the children.

穏やかで年配のお隣さんが、子どもたちにナツメヤシの実の入った袋をくれたの。

☐ sedate［形］落ち着いた、穏やかな
☐ neighbor［名］隣人、近所の人
☐ date［名］ナツメヤシの実

220 fuss [fʌ́s] | fuse [fjúːz]

Don't fuss! It's just a blown fuse.

騒がないで！ ヒューズがとんだだけだ。

☐ fuss［動］やきもきする、騒ぐ（She *fusses* too much about her daughter. 彼女は娘のことで騒ぎすぎだ）
☐ blown［形］（ヒューズが）とんだ
☐ fuse［名］電気ヒューズ、（爆弾などの）信管

絵を見ながら Listen to the English!

発音やつづりが似た単語を、まとめて体で覚えよう！

解説は次ページ

221 ensure　leisure

222 err　error

223 rarely　barely

224 division　vision

ensure, leisure / err, error / rarely, barely / division, vision

221 ensure [enʃúər] | leisure [líːʒər]

Extracurricular activities are fine, but you need to ensure that he has enough leisure time.

課外活動もよいけれど、彼の自由になる時間を確保してあげる必要がある。

- extracurricular activity　課外活動、部活
- ensure［動］〜を確実にする、確保する、保証する
- leisure［形］暇な / leisure time　暇な時間

222 err [ə́ːr] | error [érər]

To err is human, so it's no wonder so many disasters are caused by human error.

間違えるのが人間だから、人間の過失によってこれだけ多くの惨事が起きるのも不思議ではない。

- err［動］間違う、誤る
- disaster［名］災害、大惨事
- error［名］間違い、過失

223 rarely [réərli] | barely [béərli]

We rarely eat out as we barely have enough money to make ends meet.

私たちはぎりぎりで生活をやりくりしているので、めったに外食しない。

- rarely［副］めったに〜しない
- barely［副］かろうじて、ほとんど〜ない
- make ends meet　生活の収支を合わせる、やりくりする

224 division [divíʒən] | vision [víʒən]

I work in the export division, exporting high-vision TVs.

僕はハイビジョンのテレビを輸出する部門で働いています。

- export［名］輸出　［動］〜を輸出する
- division［名］部門
- vision［名］画像、映像

絵を見ながら **Listen to the English!**
発音やつづりが似た単語を、まとめて体で覚えよう！

解説は次ページ

225 heel　reel

226 impulsion　compulsion

227 institution　constitution

228 insolent　insolvent

heel, reel / impulsion, compulsion / institution, constitution / insolent, insolvent

225 heel [híːl] | reel [ríːl]

Walking in high heels would make my head reel.
ハイヒールを履くと頭がくらくらするの。

- □ heel [名] かかと / □ high heel ハイヒール
- □ reel [動] ふらふらする、よろめく、動揺する

226 impulsion [impʌ́lʃən] | compulsion [kəmpʌ́lʃən]

When she feels the impulsion to escape from life, she gets a compulsion to go shopping.
彼女は現実から逃避したいという欲求を感じると、衝動的に買い物がしたくなる。

- □ impulsion [名] 衝動、推進力
- □ escape [動] 逃げる、脱出する
- □ compulsion [名] 衝動、強制

227 institution [ìnstətjúːʃən] | constitution [kànstətjúːʃən]

All institutions are governed by the constitution.
すべての機関が憲法に基づいて統治されている。

- □ institution [名] 団体、機関
- □ be governed by 〜に支配される、管理される
- □ constitution [名] 憲法、規約

228 insolent [ínsələnt] | insolvent [insʌ́lvənt | -sɔ́l-]

Not so long ago he used to be an insolent millionaire, but now he's an insolvent beggar.
彼は少し前まで横柄な大金持ちだったけど、今では破産してこじきよ。

- □ insolent [形] 横柄な、無礼な
- □ insolvent [形] 支払い不能の
- □ millionaire [名] 百万長者
- □ beggar [名] 物ごい

絵を見ながら Listen to the English!

track 58 　解説は次ページ

発音やつづりが似た単語を、まとめて体で覚えよう！

229 replete　complete

230 hell　hello

231 wedge　edge

232 case　chaste　chase

replete, complete / hell, hello / wedge, edge / case, chaste, chase

229 replete [riplíːt] | complete [kəmplíːt]

One last chapter, replete with maps, will complete my book.

地図がたくさん入った最後の章で、私の本は完成するんだよ。

- □ chapter [名] 章
- □ replete with 〜に満ちた、〜で一杯の、満腹した
- □ complete [動] 〜を完成させる、完全なものにする

230 hell [hél] | hello [helóu]

Hey, what the hell are you two laughing about? I merely said hello to her.

おい、お前たち2人はいったい何を笑っているんだ？ オレは彼女にこんにちはと言っただけだ。

- □ hell [名] 地獄 / □ what the hell いったい
- □ merely [副] ただ、単に
- □ hello [名] 「やあ、こんにちは」という呼びかけ

231 wedge [wédʒ] | edge [édʒ]

I'll place this wedge under the edge of the door to hold it open.

閉まらないように、ドアの端にこのくさびを差し込んでおくよ。

- □ wedge [名] くさび
- □ edge [名] 端、縁

232 case [kéis] | chaste [tʃéist] | chase [tʃéis]

In any case, young women are expected to remain chaste despite being chased by young men.

ともかく、若い娘は若い男に追いかけ回されても貞淑であることが求められるのよ。

- □ in any case どんな場合でも
- □ remain [動] 〜の状態でいる
- □ despite [前] 〜にもかかわらず
- □ be expected to 〜と期待されている
- □ chaste [形] 貞淑な、純潔な
- □ chase [動] 〜を追いかける

絵を見ながら **Listen to the English!**
発音やつづりが似た単語を、まとめて体で覚えよう！

解説は次ページ

233 lubricate　lubricant

234 criteria　bacteria

235 friction　fraction

236 installation　distillation

233 lubricate [lúːbrəkèit] | lubricant [lúːbrikənt]

Lubricate all the engine's moving parts with **lubricant** before you start it again.

エンジンを再スタートする前に、すべての可動部分に潤滑油をさしてなめらかにしなさい。

- □ lubricate ［動］〜に潤滑油をさす
- □ lubricant ［名］潤滑油、潤滑剤

234 criteria [kraitíəriə] | bacteria [bæktíəriə]

Do we really have the correct **criteria** to judge what **bacteria** are good for humans?

どのバクテリアが人間にとっていいものかを判断する正しい基準を、われわれは本当に持っているのだろうか。

- □ criteria ［名］判断基準
- □ judge ［動］〜を判断する
- □ bacteria ［名］バクテリア、細菌

235 friction [frík∫ən] | fraction [fræk∫ən]

There is sure to be a lot of **friction** if you insist on 3rd graders learning **fractions**.

3年生が分数を学ぶべきだと主張すれば、必ず摩擦が起きるだろう。

- □ friction ［名］抵抗、摩擦、不和
- □ insist on 〜を強く主張する
- □ fraction ［名］分数

236 installation [ìnstəléi∫ən] | distillation [dìstəléi∫ən]

The **installation** of the new **distillation** plant may take several weeks.

この蒸留施設の設置には、数週間かかるかもしれません。

- □ installation ［名］取り付け、導入
- □ distillation ［名］蒸留 / □ distillation plant　蒸留施設

絵を見ながら **Listen to the English!**
発音やつづりが似た単語を、まとめて体で覚えよう！

解説は次ページ

237 fumble　tumble

238 dove　love　glove

239 moan　loan

240 create　cream

Day 7

fumble, tumble / dove, love, glove / moan, loan / create, cream

237 fumble [fÁmbl] | tumble [tÁmbl]

Fumbling about in her handbag for her key, all of a sudden, she found herself tumbling down the stairs.

手探りでハンドバッグの中の鍵を探すうちに、彼女は突然階段を転がり落ちた。

- □ fumble［動］手探りする
- □ all of a sudden　突然
- □ tumble［動］転ぶ、倒れる / □ tumble down the stairs　階段を転がり落ちる

238 dove [dÁv] | love [lÁv] | glove [glÁv]

He's really a dove, but on occasion, he loves to pull on the boxing gloves.

彼は本当に平和的な人だけど、時々ボクシングのグラブをつけるのも好きなの。

- □ dove［名］ハト、柔和な人　　　□ on occasion　時々
- □ love［動］〜が大好きである　　□ pull on　身に着ける
- □ boxing glove　ボクシング用のグラブ

239 moan [móun] | loan [lóun]

Stop your moaning. That is the loan you wanted, isn't it?

不平を言うのは止めてください。あなたが望んだローンでしょう。

- □ moan［動］不満を言う、嘆く、うめく
- □ loan［名］融資、借金、ローン

240 create [kriéit] | cream [kríːm]

He says he's created a new way to keep cream fresh without refrigeration.

彼は冷やさずにクリームを新鮮に保つ新しい方法を編み出したと言っている。

- □ create［動］〜を作る、創造する
- □ cream［名］クリーム
- □ refrigeration［名］冷却、冷凍

track 61 絵を見ながら **Listen to the English!**
解説は次ページ
発音やつづりが似た単語を、まとめて体で覚えよう！

241 | lump　hump

242 | evaluate　evacuate

243 | appreciate　appropriate

244 | interest　disinterest

149

lump, hump / evaluate, evacuate / appreciate, appropriate / interest, disinterest

241 lump [lʌ́mp] | hump [hʌ́mp]

The lump on the back of the camel is called a hump.

ラクダの背中のこぶは背こぶって言うんだよ。

□ lump［名］こぶ
□ camel［名］ラクダ
□ hump［名］（ラクダなどの）背こぶ

242 evaluate [ivǽljuèit] | evacuate [ivǽkjuèit]

We haven't had time to evaluate the losses yet. We are still trying to evacuate the residents.

被害を見積もる余裕はまだありません。今も住民を避難させようと努めています。

□ evaluate［動］〜を査定する　　□ loss［名］損失
□ evacuate［動］〜を避難させる　□ resident［名］居住者

243 appreciate [əpríːʃièit] | appropriate [əpróupriət]

I appreciate your kind offer, but it's not appropriate for me to take you up on it.

寛大なお申し出に感謝しますが、お受けするわけにはいきません。

□ appreciate［動］〜に感謝する、〜を高く評価する
□ appropriate［形］ふさわしい、適切な
□ take someone up on　（人）の〜に応じる

244 interest [íntərəst] | disinterest [disíntərist]

She's always interested in love stories and disinterested in war stories.

彼女はいつだってラブ・ストーリーに興味はあるけれど、戦争ものには無関心なんだ。

□ interest［名］興味 / □ interested［形］関心のある
□ disinterest［名］無関心 / □ disinterested［形］関心のない

track 62 絵を見ながら **Listen to the English!**
解説は次ページ
発音やつづりが似た単語を、まとめて体で覚えよう！

245 deserve conserve

246 invest divest

247 kidney kid

248 bash dash cash

245 deserve [dizə́ːrv] | conserve [kənsə́ːrv]

Perhaps we deserved this disaster since we still haven't learned to conserve our forests.

私たちはいまだに森林を保護できるようにならないのだから、この災害は当然の報いかもしれない。

□ deserve［動］〜を受けるに値する
□ conserve［動］（自然などを）保護する

246 invest [invést] | divest [divést]

He had secretly invested company profits overseas before he was discovered and divested of his powers.

私たちが彼のやっていたことを暴き、彼から権力を剥奪するまで、彼は密かに会社の利益を海外に投資していた。

□ invest［動］〜を投資する　　□ profit［名］利益
□ discover［動］〜を発見する　□ divest［動］〜を剥奪する

247 kidney [kídni] | kid [kíd]

She donated one of her kidneys to her kid.

彼女は腎臓のひとつを自分の子どもに提供しました。

□ donate［動］〜を提供する、贈与する
□ kidney［名］腎臓
□ kid［名］子ども

248 bash [bǽʃ] | dash [dǽʃ] | cash [kǽʃ]

He's bashing his head against a brick wall, dashing around trying to make some cash to pay his bills.

彼は請求を支払うために走り回り、レンガの壁に頭を打ちつけている。

□ bash［動］〜をぶん殴る / □ bash one's head against　〜に頭をぶつける
□ dash［動］突進する
□ cash［名］現金

track 63 絵を見ながら **Listen to the English!**
発音やつづりが似た単語を、まとめて体で覚えよう！

解説は次ページ

249 creed　breed

250 jail　bail

251 contention　intention

252 include　exclude

creed, breed / jail, bail / contention, intention / include, exclude

249 creed [kríːd] | breed [bríːd]

Forcing people of different creeds to live together can easily breed violence.

信条の異なる人々を無理に共生させれば、容易に暴力を引き起こしかねない。

- creed［名］信条、主義
- breed［動］〜を引き起こす、産む（They *breed* like rabbits. 彼らはうさぎのように繁殖する）

250 jail [dʒéil] | bail [béil]

He is in jail now, waiting for me to bail him out.

彼は今刑務所にいて、私に保釈してもらうのを待っている。

- jail［名］拘置所、刑務所
- bail ... out （人を）保釈してもらう

251 contention [kənténʃən] | intention [inténʃən]

It was his contention that he had no intention of hurting her feelings.

彼女の気持ちを傷つけるつもりはなかった、というのが彼の主張だった。

- contention［名］主張、論争
- intention［名］意図、意思 / have no intention to 〜するつもりがない
- hurt［動］〜を傷つける

252 include [inklúːd] | exclude [iksklúːd]

Room and board is $500 a week, including two meals but excluding phone charges.

部屋代と食事代は1週間で500ドルで、2食分の食費込みだけど電話代は別だよ。

- room and board　部屋代と食事代
- include［動］〜を含める / including［前］〜を含めて
- exclude［動］〜を除く / excluding［前］〜を除いて

Day 8

Keywords for Day 8

- **track 64**: excuse, exclusive / expert, expertise / compliment, complement / dissect, insect
- **track 65**: degenerate, generate / breathe, breath / divert, diver / daft, raft
- **track 66**: complex, perplex / avenue, venue / subsequently, consequently / fate, fete
- **track 67**: bide, bid / flexibility, feasibility / assert, desert / dessert, desert
- **track 68**: band, ban / intention, extension / direct, misdirect / whip, hip
- **track 69**: distribute, attribute / flatter, flatten / flutter, flatter / delude, elude
- **track 70**: rare, bare / rosy, cosy / chick, chic / explain, plain
- **track 71**: belle, ball, bell / average, leverage / cord, core / consent, assent
- **track 72**: gasp, grasp / fold, folk / insert, inert / credit, discredit

絵を見ながら Listen to the English!
発音やつづりが似た単語を、まとめて体で覚えよう！

track 64

解説は次ページ

253 excuse　exclusive

254 expert　expertise

255 compliment　complement

256 dissect　insect

excuse, exclusive / expert, expertise / compliment, complement / dissect, insect

253 excuse [ikskjúːz] | exclusive [iksklúːsiv]

Excuse me. You did say this was the most exclusive hotel in the city, didn't you?

すみません。ここがこの町で最高級のホテルだと言いましたよね？

- excuse me　すみません
- exclusive［形］高級な、限定された（This car is for the president's *exclusive* use. この車は大統領が乗るときだけに使われる車です）

254 expert [ékspəːrt] | expertise [èkspərtíːz]

He's an economic expert with plenty of business expertise.

彼は商取引の専門知識を豊富に持っている経済学の権威です。

- expert［名］専門家（economic *expert* 経済学の専門家）
- plenty of　たくさんの〜
- expertise［名］専門的知識

255 compliment [kámpləmənt] | complement [kámpləmənt]

I know he likes to fish for compliments, but the wine he chose this time did complement the food perfectly.

彼がほめられるのが好きなのは知っているけど、今回彼が選んだワインは料理にぴったりだった。

- compliment［名］ほめ言葉、お世辞 / □ fish for compliment　相手にお世辞を言わせようとする
- complement［動］〜を補完する、引き立たせる

256 dissect [disékt | dai-] | insect [ínsekt]

My son likes to dissect the insects that he catches.

息子は自分で捕まえた虫を解剖するのが好きなのよ。

- dissect［動］〜を解剖する、細かく調べる
- insect［名］昆虫

track 65 絵を見ながら **Listen to the English!**
発音やつづりが似た単語を、まとめて体で覚えよう！

解説は次ページ

257 degenerate　generate

258 breathe　breath

259 divert　diver

260 daft　raft

degenerate, generate / breathe, breath / divert, diver / daft, raft

257 degenerate [didʒénərèit] | generate [dʒénərèit]

Their argument soon degenerated into a fight that generated a lot of damage to our property.

彼らの議論はすぐに争いへと堕落し、私たちの所有物に多大な損害を与えた。

□ argument［名］議論、主張　　□ degenerate into 　〜へ堕落する
□ generate［動］〜を引き起こす　□ property［名］所有物、財産

258 breathe [bríːð] | breath [bréθ]

You can't breathe in water, so you have to hold your breath while diving.

水の中では呼吸ができないから、潜水している間は息を止めなければならない。

□ breathe［動］呼吸する
□ breath［名］呼吸 / □ hold one's breath　息を止める
□ dive［動］潜水する、ダイビングする

259 divert [divə́ːrt | dai-] | diver [dáivər]

Nothing can divert his attention when he is training divers.

彼がダイバーたちを訓練しているときは、何事も彼の注意をそらすことはできない。

□ divert［動］〜をそらす / □ divert one's attention　（人の）注意をそらす
□ attention［名］注意
□ diver［名］水に潜る人、ダイバー

260 daft [dǽft | dɑ́ːft] | raft [rǽft | rɑ́ːft]

It's a daft idea to buy a life raft for the home.

家用に救命ボートを買うなんてばかげた考えだ。

□ daft［形］ばかげた、気のふれた（Don't be so daft! そんなばかなことはやめろ！）
□ raft［名］いかだ / □ life raft　救命ボート

絵を見ながら **Listen to the English!**
発音やつづりが似た単語を、まとめて体で覚えよう！

解説は次ページ

261 complex　perplex

262 avenue　venue

263 subsequently　consequently

264 fate　fete

complex, perplex / avenue, venue / subsequently, consequently / fate, fete

261 complex [kəmpléks] | perplex [pərpléks]

Such complex questions absolutely perplex me.
そういう複雑な問題にはまったく困ってしまう。

- complex ［形］複雑な
- absolutely ［副］完全に、すっかり
- perplex ［動］〜を当惑させる（*perplexing* problem 厄介な問題）

262 avenue [ǽvənjùː] | venue [vénjuː]

Just walk along 41st Avenue and you'll be at the venue in 15 minutes.
41番街をずっと歩いていけば、15分で会場に着くよ。

- avenue ［名］大通り、《A-》〜街
- venue ［名］現場、会場（a change of *venue* 開催地の変更）

263 subsequently [sʌ́bsikwəntli] | consequently [kɑ́nsəkwəntli]

Though the bank promised to give the company a loan, it subsequently reneged, and consequently, the company went bankrupt.
銀行が融資すると約束した後に約束が破られ、結果的に会社は倒産した。

- subsequently ［副］その後に
- consequently ［副］結果的に
- renege ［動］（約束を）破る
- go bankrupt　破産する

264 fate [féit] | fete [féit]

I learned my fate when I had a Tarot reading at the fete.
祭典のタロット占いで自分の運命を知った。

- fate ［名］運命、運
- tarot ［名］タロットカード
- fete ［名］祭典

track 67 絵を見ながら **Listen to the English!**
発音やつづりが似た単語を、まとめて体で覚えよう！

解説は次ページ

265 bide bid

266 flexibility feasibility

267 assert desert

268 dessert desert

bide, bid / flexibility, feasibility / assert, desert / dessert, desert

265 **bide** [báid] | **bid** [bíd]

He's biding his time before he makes his bid for power.

彼は権力を得るための好機を狙っている。

☐ bide［動］〜を待つ / ☐ bide one's time　好機を待つ
☐ bid［名］（〜のための）努力、入札 / ☐ make a bid for　〜のための努力をする

266 **flexibility** [flèksəbíləti] | **feasibility** [fìːzəbíləti]

We must have flexibility in order to implement the suggestions in this feasibility study.

この予備調査で推薦している事を実行に移すためには、われわれは柔軟でなければならない。

☐ flexibility［名］柔軟性　　　☐ implement［動］〜を実行する
☐ feasibility［名］実現可能性 / ☐ feasibility study　予備調査

267 **assert** [əsə́ːrt] | **desert** [dizə́ːrt]

Though I asserted my innocence and was found not guilty, all my friends deserted me.

私は無実を主張して無罪が判明したのに、友人はみんな私を見放した。

☐ assert［動］〜を断言する、力説する
☐ innocence［名］無罪
☐ guilty［形］有罪の
☐ desert［動］〜を見捨てる

268 **dessert** [dizə́ːrt] | **desert** [dizə́ːrt]

Faced with the lovely dessert all my good intentions suddenly deserted me.

目の前においしそうなデザートが現れて、私の立派な心構えは突如どこかへ消えてしまった。

☐ face［動］〜に直面する　　　☐ dessert［名］デザート
☐ intention［名］意図　　　　　☐ desert［動］〜から去る

track 68 絵を見ながら **Listen to the English!**
発音やつづりが似た単語を、まとめて体で覚えよう！

解説は次ページ

269	band　ban
270	intention　extension
271	direct　misdirect
272	whip　hip

269 band [bǽnd] | ban [bǽn]

Playing with rubber bands during class is banned.
授業中に輪ゴムで遊ぶのは禁止されています。

- □ play with 〜で遊ぶ
- □ rubber band 輪ゴム
- □ ban［動］〜を禁止する

270 intention [inténʃən] | extension [iksténʃən]

I have no intention of building an extension to this house yet.
まだこの家を建て増しするつもりはないよ。

- □ intention［名］意図（He's full of good *intention*, but can't really do anything to help. 彼は善意に溢れているが、何も役に立つことができない）
- □ extension［名］建て増し、延長

271 direct [dirékt] | misdirect [mìsdirékt]

I asked the boy the most direct way to the station, but he purposely misdirected me.
少年に駅までの最短路を聞いたが、彼はわざと間違った道を教えた。

- □ direct［形］一直線の、まっすぐな
- □ purposely［副］わざと、故意に
- □ misdirect［動］〜に間違って教える

272 whip [hwíp] | hip [híp]

To crack the whip you must swivel your hips.
ムチをピシッと鳴らしたいのなら、腰を回さないといけないよ。

- □ whip［名］むち / □ crack a whip むちをピシッと鳴らす
- □ swivel［動］〜を回転させる
- □ hip［名］腰

track 69

絵を見ながら **Listen to the English!**
発音やつづりが似た単語を、まとめて体で覚えよう！

解説は次ページ

| 273 | distribute　attribute |

| 274 | flatter　flatten |

| 275 | flutter　flatter |

| 276 | delude　elude |

distribute, attribute / flatter, flatten / flutter, flatter / delude, elude

273 distribute [distríbju:t] | attribute [ətríbju:t]

As he distributed the prizes to the winners, he attributed their success to their hard work.

彼は受賞者に賞を授与しながら、この成功は彼らの努力の結果だと述べた。

- □ distribute［動］〜を分配する、配布する（He is *distributing* leaflets to the crowd. 彼はビラを群衆に配っている）
- □ attribute A to B　AをBのおかげだと考える

274 flatter [flǽtər] | flatten [flǽtn]

It is those who flatter you today who may flatten you tomorrow.

今日あなたを褒めちぎっている人たちこそ、明日あなたをがっかりさせる人々かもしれない。

- □ flatter［動］〜にお世辞を言う（*flattering* remarks お世辞の言葉）
- □ flatten［動］〜をがっかりさせる、平らにする（The rabbit was *flattened* by a passing car. うさぎは通りがかった車にぺちゃんこにされた）

275 flutter [flʌ́tər] | flatter [flǽtər]

She fluttered her eyelashes at the young man who was flattering her on her cooking.

料理のお世辞を言う若い男に、彼女はウインクをした。

- □ flutter［動］〜をはためかす / □ flutter one's eye lashes　ウインクする
- □ flatter［動］〜にお世辞を言って褒める

276 delude [dilú:d] | elude [ilú:d]

Don't delude yourself; there's no way to elude your financial problems.

自分をごまかすなよ。金銭の問題から逃れられる道はないんだから。

- □ delude［動］（人に）信じ込ませる、（人を）騙す / □ delude oneself　思い違いをする
- □ elude［動］〜を回避する

絵を見ながら Listen to the English!

発音やつづりが似た単語を、まとめて体で覚えよう！

track 70

解説は次ページ

277 rare bare

278 rosy cosy

279 chick chic

280 explain plain

277 rare [réər] | bare [béər]

It's rare to see city people walking around in bare feet.
都会の人が裸足で歩く姿を目にするのは珍しいね。

- □ rare［形］珍しい、まれな（It's *rare* for him to be late. 彼が遅れるなんて珍しい）
- □ bare［形］裸の、むきだしの / □ bare feet　裸足 / □ bare hands　素手

278 rosy [róuzi] | cosy [kóuzi]

The old man still remembers her rosy cheeks and their first cozy little house.
老人はまだ、彼女の血色のよいほおや、初めて一緒に住んだ居心地のよい小さな家を覚えている。

- □ rosy［形］血色のよい、ばら色の
- □ cheek［名］ほお
- □ cozy［形］居心地のよい

279 chick [tʃík] | chic [ʃí(ː)k]

She put three little chicks on her chic little hat.
彼女は自分の小さいおしゃれな帽子の上に、3 羽の小さなひよこを置いた。

- □ chick［名］ひよこ
- □ chic［形］しゃれた、粋な
- □ hat［名］（縁のある）帽子

280 explain [ikspléin] | plain [pléin]

The teacher explained why there is such a great plain in the center of America.
先生はこのような広大な平原がアメリカの真ん中にある理由を説明した。

- □ explain［動］〜を説明する
- □ plain［名］平原、平野

track 71 絵を見ながら **Listen to the English!**
発音やつづりが似た単語を、まとめて体で覚えよう！

解説は次ページ

281　belle　ball　bell

282　average　leverage

283　cord　core

284　consent　assent

belle, ball, bell / average, leverage / cord, core / consent, assent

281 **belle**[bél] | **ball**[bɔ́ːl] | **bell**[bél]

The belle of the ball promised to give me one of her bells.

舞踏会にいた美女が、僕にベルをひとつくれると約束したんだ。

- □ belle ［名］美人
- □ ball ［名］舞踏会
- □ bell ［名］ベル、鐘

282 **average**[ǽvəridʒ] | **leverage**[lévəridʒ]

The average size of the rocks was 2 meters in diameter, so we had to use leverage to move them.

岩の大きさは平均直径2メートルもあったので、動かすためには、てこの作用を使わなければならなかった。

- □ average ［形］平均の
- □ diameter ［名］直径
- □ rock ［名］岩
- □ leverage ［名］てこの作用

283 **cord**[kɔ́ːrd] | **core**[kɔ́ːr]

That girl in the cord skirt over there threw the apple core on the ground.

あそこにいるコーデュロイのスカートをはいた女の子が、りんごの芯を地面に放り投げたんだよ。

- □ cord skirt コーデュロイのスカート
- □ core ［名］芯

284 **consent**[kənsént] | **assent**[əsént]

Should you consent to my proposal, he would also assent to it.

あなたが私の計画に同意してくれたら、彼も賛成してくれるでしょう。

- □ consent ［動］同意する、応じる
- □ proposal ［名］提案、企画案、計画
- □ assent to ～に同意する、賛成する

track 72 絵を見ながら **Listen to the English!**
発音やつづりが似た単語を、まとめて体で覚えよう！

解説は次ページ

285 gasp　grasp

286 fold　folk

287 insert　inert

288 credit　discredit

gasp, grasp / fold, folk / insert, inert / credit, discredit

285 **gasp** [gǽsp | gάːsp] | **grasp** [grǽsp | grάːsp]

We all gasped with amazement as, at the last second, he grasped the rope with both hands.

最後の瞬間に彼が両手でロープをつかんだとき、私たちは息をのんだ。

□ gasp［動］あえぐ、ハッと息をのむ
□ amazement［名］驚き
□ grasp［動］〜を（しっかり）握る

286 **fold** [fóuld] | **folk** [fóuk]

He likes to fold his arms when he sings his favorite folk songs.

彼はお気に入りのフォークソングを歌うとき、腕を組むのが好きだ。

□ fold［動］〜を組む、折る
□ favorite［形］お気に入りの
□ folk［形］民間の、民俗の / □ folk song 民謡、フォークソング

287 **insert** [insə́ːrt] | **inert** [inə́ːrt]

Upon inserting the key in the lock and opening the door, he discovered her inert on the floor.

彼が鍵を錠にさしてドアを開けると、床で動けなくなっている彼女を発見した。

□ insert［動］〜を挿入する
□ lock［名］錠
□ inert［形］自力で行動できない

288 **credit** [krédit] | **discredit** [diskrédit]

He is a credit to our family and has never done anything to discredit our reputation.

彼は私たち一族の誇りで、我が家の名声に傷つけたことは一度もない。

□ credit［名］名誉、信用
□ discredit［動］〜の信用を傷つける
□ reputation［名］評判、名声

Day 9

Keywords for Day 9

- **track 73**: dispute, disrepute / bear, blare / bus, burst, bust / lapse, collapse
- **track 74**: bawl, ball, / borrow, barrow / bear, bare / heel, heal
- **track 75**: involve, evolve / installation, installment / insist, subsist / fail, jail
- **track 76**: hare, rare / date, gate / candid, candidate / indicate, abdicate
- **track 77**: book, nook / compound, pound / attitude, altitude / lodge, ledge
- **track 78**: capacity, capability / confine, confide / chant, enchant / claim, reclaim
- **track 79**: excursion, incursion / bump, dump / seclude, include / gabble, gable
- **track 80**: indication, medication / grove, grave / align, alien / rooster, booster
- **track 81**: broom, bloom / gift, gist / cuddle, huddle / fancy, fan

track 73 絵を見ながら **Listen to the English!**
発音やつづりが似た単語を、まとめて体で覚えよう！

解説は次ページ

289	dispute　disrepute

290	bear　blare

291	bus　burst　bust

292	lapse　collapse

289 dispute [dispjúːt] | disrepute [dìsripjúːt]

Such a dispute would bring our company into disrepute.

そのような論争は、わが社に悪評をもたらすだろう。

- □ dispute ［名］論争、議論
- □ disrepute ［目］悪評、不名誉 / □ bring...into disrepute …に悪評をもたらす

290 bear [béər] | blare [bléər]

I just can't bear the blare of this brass band.

このブラスバンドの騒音には耐えられない。

- □ bear ［動］〜に耐える
- □ blare ［名］（らっぱなどの）騒々しい音
- □ brass band　ブラスバンド、吹奏楽団

291 bus [bÁs] | burst [bə́ːrst] | bust [bÁst]

The bus tire burst, leaving busted pieces spread all over the road.

バスのタイヤがパンクし、道路中に破片が撒き散らされた。

- □ bus ［名］バス
- □ busted ［形］壊れた
- □ burst ［動］破裂する、爆発する
- □ spread ［動］散らばる

292 lapse [lǽps] | collapse [kəlǽps]

Even a short lapse in concentration can make your whole game plan collapse.

少しでも集中力が途切れると、ゲームの作戦がすべて破たんするおそれがある。

- □ lapse ［名］ささいな間違い、過失
- □ concentration ［名］集中力、専念
- □ collapse ［動］つぶれる、崩壊する

絵を見ながら Listen to the English!
track 74
発音やつづりが似た単語を、まとめて体で覚えよう！
解説は次ページ

293　bawl　ball

294　borrow　barrow

295　bear　bare

296　heel　heal

Day 9

bawl, ball / borrow, barrow / bear, bare / heel, heal

293 bawl [bɔ́:l] | ball [bɔ́:l]

The little boy started to bawl when his ball went over the wall.

小さな男の子のボールが壁を越えてしまうと、その子は泣きだした。

- □ bawl［動］大声で叫ぶ、泣く
- □ ball［名］球、ボール
- □ wall［名］壁、塀

294 borrow [bárou | bɔ́r-] | barrow [bǽrou]

Can I borrow your barrow, please?

君の手押し車を貸してもらえるかい?

- □ borrow［動］〜を借りる
- □ barrow［名］一輪手押し車

295 bear [béər] | bare [béər]

Do bears bare their teeth when they are angry?

クマは怒ったときに歯をむき出すの?

- □ bear［名］クマ
- □ bare［動］〜をあらわにする / □ bare one's teeth　歯をむき出す
- □ angry［形］腹を立てた

296 heel [hí:l] | heal [hí:l]

I fell down the ladder and cut my heel, but it's still not healed.

はしごから落ちてかかとを切ってしまったが、まだ治らない。

- □ ladder［名］はしご
- □ heel［名］かかと
- □ heal［動］〜を治す、癒す

絵を見ながら **Listen to the English!**
発音やつづりが似た単語を、まとめて体で覚えよう！

解説は次ページ

297 involve　evolve

298 installation　installment

299 insist　subsist

300 fail　jail

involve, evolve / installation, installment / insist, subsist / fail, jail

297 involve [inválv] | evolve [iválv]

He involved the staff in the reform plan, and eventually they evolved a new system to run the company.

彼は改革計画にスタッフを巻き込み、ついには会社を運営する新しいシステムを発展させた。

- □ involve [動] 〜を巻き込む
- □ eventually [副] 結局は、やがて
- □ reform plan　改革案
- □ evolve [動] 〜を発展させる

298 installation [ìnstəléiʃən] | installment [instɔ́ːlmənt]

We can pay the installation fee by installment, too.

取り付ける費用は、分割払いでも支払えるのよ。

- □ installation [名] 取り付け、（プログラムの）インストール
- □ fee [名] 手数料、費用
- □ installment [名] 分割払いの1回分

299 insist [insíst] | subsist [səbsíst]

He insisted that people could subsist on $25 a week if they budgeted their money.

彼は、人々が予算を立てて使えば1週間を25ドルで生活できると主張した。

- □ insist [動] 〜を強く主張する、〜と言い張る
- □ subsist on　〜で生計を立てる
- □ budget [動] 〜の予算を組む、（時間・資金などを）割り当てる

300 fail [féil] | jail [dʒéil]

If we fail, we'll land in jail.

もし失敗すれば、俺たちは刑務所行きだ。

- □ fail [動] 失敗する
- □ land in　（悪い状況に）陥る
- □ jail [名] 刑務所、留置所

track 76 　絵を見ながら **Listen to the English!**
解説は次ページ
発音やつづりが似た単語を、まとめて体で覚えよう！

301 hare　rare

302 date　gate

303 candid　candidate

304 indicate　abdicate

hare, rare / date, gate / candid, candidate / indicate, abdicate

301 hare [héər] | rare [réər]

Hares are rare around here nowadays, but if you are patient you might see one.
最近、この辺りでは野ウサギは珍しいけど、忍耐強ければ見られるかもしれない。

- □ hare [名] 野ウサギ
- □ rare [形] 珍しい、まれな
- □ patient [形] 忍耐強い

302 date [déit] | gate [géit]

I'm meeting my date by the school gate tonight.
今夜、デートの相手と校門で会うことになっているんだ。

- □ date [名] デートの相手
- □ gate [名] 門、入り口

303 candid [kǽndid] | candidate [kǽndidèit | -dət]

I like his candid attitude; I think he's the right candidate for mayor.
私は彼の率直な態度が好きです。彼こそ市長にふさわしい候補者だと思います。

- □ candid [形] 率直な、公正な
- □ right [形] 適した
- □ mayor [名] 市長
- □ attitude [名] 態度、姿勢
- □ candidate [名] 候補者

304 indicate [índikèit] | abdicate [ǽbdəkèit]

The king indicated that he would abdicate the throne in the near future.
王は近い将来、退位するつもりだと述べた。

- □ indicate [動] 〜だと知らせる、〜を述べる
- □ abdicate [動] 放棄する / □ abdicate the throne （王が）退位する
- □ near future 近い未来

絵を見ながら **Listen to the English!**
発音やつづりが似た単語を、まとめて体で覚えよう！

解説は次ページ

305 book　nook

306 compound　pound

307 attitude　altitude

308 lodge　ledge

book, nook / compound, pound / attitude, altitude / lodge, ledge

305 book [búk] | nook [núk]

He's reading a book in the shady nook in the garden.

彼は日陰になっている庭の隅で本を読んでいる。

- □ book [名] 本、書物
- □ shady [形] 日陰の
- □ nook [名] 隅、隠れ場所

306 compound [kámpaund] | pound [páund]

With compound interest, I estimate you'll get one more pound per annum.

複利で見積もると、1年ごとに1ポンドずつ増えますよ。

- □ compound [形] 複数の部分からなる / □ compound interest （単利に対して）複利
- □ estimate [動] 〜を見積もる　　□ pound [名] ポンド
- □ per annum　1年につき

307 attitude [ǽtitjùːd] | altitude [ǽltətjùːd]

A person's attitude toward life is greatly influenced by their social altitude.

人の人生に対する態度には、社会的地位の高さがに大いに影響している。

- □ attitude [名] 態度、姿勢
- □ influenced by　〜に影響される
- □ altitude [名] 高さ、標高 / □ social altitude　社会的地位の高さ

308 lodge [ládʒ] | ledge [lédʒ]

He lodged the insurance claim as soon as he learned his ship had hit a ledge.

彼は自分の船が岩礁にぶつかったと知るや、保険金の請求を申し立てた。

- □ lodge [動] 〜を提出する、申し立てる
- □ insurance claim　保険金請求
- □ ledge [名] 岩礁

絵を見ながら **Listen to the English!**
発音やつづりが似た単語を、まとめて体で覚えよう！

解説は次ページ

309 capacity capability

310 confine confide

311 chant enchant

312 claim reclaim

309 capacity [kəpǽsəti] | capability [kèipəbíləti]

If we run at full capacity, we have the capability to double our output.
私たちには、全力で稼働すれば生産高を2倍にする力があります。

- □ capacity［名］生産能力、性能
- □ double［動］〜を2倍にする
- □ capability［名］能力、才能
- □ output［名］生産高

310 confine [kənfáin] | confide [kənfáid]

I've been confined to bed with a cold for the past week, and I've got no one to confide in.
この1週間風邪で寝込んでいて、秘密を打ち明けられる人がいなかった。

- □ confine［動］〜を制限する / □ confined to bed 病床にある
- □ confide［動］秘密を打ち明ける（He confided to me that he had spent 5 years in prison. 彼は私に5年間監獄で過ごしたことを打ち明けた）

311 chant [tʃǽnt] | enchant [intʃǽnt | -tʃɑ́:nt]

She found the monks' chanting enchanting.
彼女は僧たちの詠唱に魅了された。

- □ monk［名］僧
- □ chant［動］歌う、詠唱する
- □ enchant［動］〜を魅了する / □ enchanting［形］魅惑的な

312 claim [kléim] | reclaim [rikléim]

He claims he is entitled to reclaim some of the tax he paid last year.
彼は昨年払った税金のいくらかを取り戻す資格があると主張している。

- □ claim［動］〜を主張する
- □ be entitled to 〜する資格がある
- □ reclaim［動］〜の返還を要求する

track 79 絵を見ながら **Listen to the English!**
発音やつづりが似た単語を、まとめて体で覚えよう！

解説は次ページ

313 excursion　incursion

314 bump　dump

315 seclude　include

316 gabble　gable

excursion, incursion / bump, dump / seclude, include / gabble, gable

313 excursion [ikskə́ːrʒən] | incursion [inkə́ːrʒən]

We were setting out on a weekend excursion when the incursion occurred.

その襲撃が起きたとき、私たちは週末の小旅行に出かけようとしていた。

- □ set out on　～に出発する
- □ excursion［名］小旅行
- □ incursion［名］襲撃

314 bump [bʌ́mp] | dump [dʌ́mp]

Last night our car bumped into a pile of rubbish that someone had dumped on the road.

昨夜、誰かが道に捨てたゴミの山にわれわれの車が突っ込んだ。

- □ bump into　～と衝突する
- □ rubbish［名］ごみ
- □ pile［名］大量、積み重ね
- □ dump［動］～を投げ捨てる

315 seclude [siklúːd] | include [inklúːd]

He actually prefers the secluded life and refuses to see anyone, including his wife.

実際、彼は隠遁生活の方が好きで、奥さんも含めて人と会うのを嫌がる。

- □ prefer［動］～を好む
- □ seclude［動］～を締め出す / □ secluded［形］人里離れた、隠遁した
- □ include［動］～を含める / □ including［前］～を含めて

316 gabble [gǽbl] | gable [géibl]

He gabbled on about how nice their new gabled patio was going to be.

彼は、新しい切り妻のあるテラスがどれだけ素晴らしくなるのか早口にまくし立てた。

- □ gabble［動］早口にしゃべる
- □ gabled［形］切り妻造りの
- □ patio［名］テラス、中庭

track 80 絵を見ながら **Listen to the English!**
発音やつづりが似た単語を、まとめて体で覚えよう！

解説は次ページ

317 indication　medication

318 grove　grave

319 align　alien

320 rooster　booster

317 indication [ìndikéiʃən] | medication [mèdəkéiʃən]

It's an indication that you're getting older when you can't get to sleep without medication.

薬なしで眠れなくなるのは、老化の兆候ですよ。

- indication ［名］兆候
- get to sleep　眠りにつく
- medication ［名］薬物治療、投薬

318 grove [gróuv] | grave [gréiv]

I was hiding in the olive grove next to the grave.

僕は、お墓の隣にあるオリーブの林に隠れていた。

- hide ［動］隠れる
- olive ［名］オリーブ
- grove ［名］林、小さい森
- grave ［名］墓

319 align [əláin] | alien [éiljən]

We should align ourselves with alien workers in their struggle for fair treatment.

私たちは、公正な扱いを求めて闘っている外国人労働者と連携すべきだ。

- align oneself with　〜と提携する
- struggle ［名］奮闘
- alien woker　外国人労働者
- fair treatment　公正な扱い

320 rooster [rúːstər] | booster [búːstər]

I don't think a new Red Rooster restaurant would be a great economic booster for our town.

新しいレッド・ルースターのレストランが、私たちの町の経済を活性化させるとは思えません。

- rooster ［名］雄鶏
- booster ［名］助力となるもの、後援者

track 81 絵を見ながら **Listen to the English!**
発音やつづりが似た単語を、まとめて体で覚えよう！

解説は次ページ

321 broom　bloom

322 gift　gist

323 cuddle　huddle

324 fancy　fan

broom, bloom / gift, gist / cuddle, huddle / fancy, fan

321 **broom** [brúːm] | **bloom** [blúːm]

We will need a new broom to clean up the garden before all the spring flowers bloom.
春の花が咲く前に庭を掃除するために、新しいほうきが必要よ。

□ broom ［名］ほうき
□ bloom ［動］咲く、開花する

322 **gift** [gíft] | **gist** [dʒíst]

I knew he was a gifted student as soon as I read the gist of his report.
彼のレポートの要点を読んですぐに、彼が有能な学生だとわかりましたよ。

□ gift ［名］贈り物 / □ gifted ［形］すぐれた才能のある
□ gist ［名］要点、骨子

323 **cuddle** [kʌ́dl] | **huddle** [hʌ́dl]

She cuddled the two little boys after finding them huddled together under the table.
テーブルの下で小さな男の子が2人身を寄せ合っているのを見つけて、彼女は彼らを抱きしめた。

□ cuddle ［動］〜を抱きしめる
□ huddle ［動］身を寄せ合う

324 **fancy** [fǽnsi] | **fan** [fǽn]

Who gave you such a fancy fan?
そんなしゃれた扇子、誰にもらったの？

□ fancy ［形］しゃれた、凝った
□ fan ［名］扇子

Day 10

Keywords for Day 10

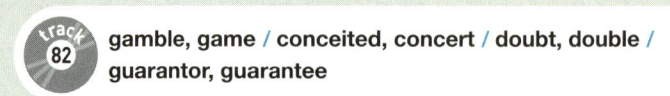

- **track 82**: gamble, game / conceited, concert / doubt, double / guarantor, guarantee
- **track 83**: thrash, crash / slack, lack / flake, lake / health, wealth
- **track 84**: have, halve, half / compel, complete / scare, care / procure, cure
- **track 85**: blanket, bracket / jeopardy, jeopardize / scandal, scanner, scan / according, accordion
- **track 86**: utter, butter / eye, cockeyed / nut, hut / hurt, hut
- **track 87**: invent, invest / do, outdo / vow, low / few, curfew
- **track 88**: congratulate, graduate / itch, pitch / grave, engrave / gross, engross
- **track 89**: enhance, hence / rough, enough / jackpot, pot / riddle, griddle
- **track 90**: main, remain / amass, mass / mayor, major / maternal, paternal

track 82

絵を見ながら **Listen to the English!**
発音やつづりが似た単語を、まとめて体で覚えよう！

解説は次ページ

325 gamble game

326 conceited concert

327 doubt double

328 guarantor guarantee

325 gamble [gǽmbl] | game [géim]

He **gambled** away all his money in the card **game**.

彼はトランプゲームで全財産を失った。

- gamble away 〜を賭け事で失う
- card game トランプゲーム

326 conceited [kənsíːtid] | concert [kάnsəːrt]

Mary became very **conceited** after her **concert** was a great success.

メアリーはコンサートを大成功させてからというもの、かなり思い上がっている。

- conceited［形］うぬぼれた、思い上がった
- concert［名］音楽会、コンサート
- great success 大成功

327 doubt [dáut] | double [dʌ́bl]

I **doubt** they can **double** their output next year.

彼らが来年の生産量を2倍に増やせるか疑問に思う。

- doubt［動］〜を疑問に思う
- double［動］〜を倍にする
- output［名］生産高

328 guarantor [gæ̀rəntɔ́ːr] | guarantee [gæ̀rəntíː]

You need a **guarantor** to **guarantee** that you will repay the loan on time.

あなたが借金を予定通りに返済できることを保証する、保証人が必要です。

- guarantor［名］保証人
- repay［動］（金を）返す
- on time 遅れずに、予定通りに
- guarantee［動］〜を保証する
- loan［名］貸付金、ローン

絵を見ながら **Listen to the English!**
発音やつづりが似た単語を、まとめて体で覚えよう！

解説は次ページ

329 thrash　crash

330 slack　lack

331 flake　lake

332 health　wealth

thrash, crash / slack, lack / flake, lake / health, wealth

329 thrash [θrǽʃ] | crash [krǽʃ]

His dad thrashed him after he crashed the family's new car.

彼が家の新車をぶつけた後に、父親は彼をむちで叩いた。

- □ thrash [動] 〜を強く打つ、むち打つ
- □ crash [動] (車を) ぶつける、壊す

330 slack [slǽk] | lack [lǽk]

In winter, business is slack for lack of customers.

冬場は客不足のせいで商売に活気がない。

- □ slack [形] 不景気な、活気のない
- □ lack [名] 不足、欠如
- □ customer [名] 顧客

331 flake [fléik] | lake [léik]

Flakes of snow fall on the lake in winter.

冬は湖に雪片がひらひらと舞い落ちる。

- □ flake [名] (雪・羽毛などの) 一片
- □ lake [名] 湖

332 health [hélθ] | wealth [wélθ]

You need to put your health above your wealth, sir.

あなたは財力よりご自分の健康を大事にしなければいけません。

- □ put A above B　AをBより優先させる
- □ health [名] 健康
- □ wealth [名] 富

track 84 絵を見ながら **Listen to the English!**
発音やつづりが似た単語を、まとめて体で覚えよう！

解説は次ページ

333 | have   halve   half

334 | compel   complete

335 | scare   care

336 | procure   cure

have, halve, half / compel, complete / scare, care / procure, cure

333 **have**[hǽv] | **halve**[hǽv | hɑ́ːv] | **half**[hǽf | hɑ́ːf]

I have to halve the apple so that I can give him half.
彼にリンゴを半分あげられるように、2等分しないといけないの。

- □ have［動］〜を持っている / □ have to 〜する必要がある
- □ halve［動］〜を半分にする
- □ half［名］半分

334 **compel**[kəmpél] | **complete**[kəmplíːt]

I'm compelled to say that I wouldn't have been able to complete the assignment without your help.
あなたの助けなしでは課題を終わらせられなかったと言うしかないわ。

- □ compel［動］（人に）無理に〜させる / □ be compelled to 〜せざるを得ない
- □ complete［動］〜を完了する
- □ assignment［名］課題、任務

335 **scare**[skɛ́ər] | **care**[kɛ́ər]

Don't be scared. I'll take care of you.
怖がらないで。僕が助けてあげるよ。

- □ scare［動］〜を怖がらせる / □ scared［形］怖がる
- □ care［名］世話 / □ take care of 〜の面倒をみる

336 **procure**[proukjúər | prə-] | **cure**[kjúər]

I procured an agreement from him that I wouldn't have to pay anything if the new cure didn't work.
新しい治療がうまくいかなかったら、私は何も支払わなくていいという同意を彼に取りつけた。

- □ procure［動］〜を手に入れる
- □ agreement［名］同意、合意
- □ cure［名］治療（法）

track 85 絵を見ながら **Listen to the English!**
発音やつづりが似た単語を、まとめて体で覚えよう！

解説は次ページ

337 blanket　bracket

338 jeopardy　jeopardize

339 scandal　scanner　scan

340 according　accordion

337 blanket [blǽŋkit] | bracket [brǽkit]

You'll find the tariff charge for these blankets in the brackets at the bottom of the page.

この毛布の関税料金は、ページの下の括弧に記載してありますよ。

□ tariff［名］関税、運賃　　□ charge［名］料金、使用料
□ blanket［名］毛布　　　　□ bracket［名］括弧

338 jeopardy [dʒépərdi] | jeopardize [dʒépərdàiz]

I won't let him put your future in jeopardy nor let his foolish behavior jeopardize your reputation.

彼にあなたの将来を危険にさらしたり、名声に傷つけたりさせません。

□ jeopardy［名］危険（にさらされること）
□ jeopardize［動］〜を危険にさらす
□ reputation［名］評判、名声

339 scandal [skǽndl] | scanner [skǽnər] | scan [skǽn]

It will be a scandal should someone discover you using the company's scanner to scan your personal papers.

私的な書類をスキャンするのに会社のスキャナーを使っているのが見つかったら、スキャンダルになるよ。

□ scandal［名］醜聞、スキャンダル
□ scanner［名］コンピュータに画像を取り込む装置、スキャナー
□ scan［動］（画像を）取り込む、〜をスキャンする

340 according [əkɔ́ːrdiŋ] | accordion [əkɔ́ːrdiən]

According to my watch it's 4 o'clock, and I've got to get you to your accordion class.

私の時計だと4時だよ。君をアコーディオンのレッスンに連れて行かないと。

□ according to　〜によると
□ get ... to　（人を）〜に運ぶ
□ accordion［名］《楽器》アコーディオン

絵を見ながら **Listen to the English!**
発音やつづりが似た単語を、まとめて体で覚えよう！

解説は次ページ

341 utter butter

342 eye cockeyed

343 nut hut

344 hurt hut

utter, butter / eye, cockeyed / nut, hut / hurt, hut

341 utter [ʌ́tər] | butter [bʌ́tər]

She's not an utter fool; she knows on which side her bread is buttered.

彼女は全くのバカというわけではない。パンのどっちの面にバターが塗られているか知っているからね。

- □ utter［形］完全な、全くの
- □ fool［名］ばか者
- □ butter［動］〜にバターを塗る

342 eye [ái] | cockeyed [kákàid]

She eyed me dubiously as I was doing my best to defend Jean's cockeyed plan.

ジーンのばかげた企画を懸命に擁護している私を、彼女は疑わしそうにじろじろ見た。

- □ eye［動］〜をじっと見る
- □ defend［動］〜を守る、擁護する
- □ dubiously［副］半信半疑に
- □ cockeyed［形］ばかな、斜視の

343 nut [nʌ́t] | hut [hʌ́t]

You're off your nut to have three meals a day at Pizza Hut!

1日3食、ピザハットで食事するなんて正気かい！

- □ be off one's nut　正気でない、頭がおかしい、混乱している
- □ meal［名］食事
- □ hut［名］小屋

344 hurt [hə́ːrt] | hut [hʌ́t]

His leg was hurt when the strong wind blew his hut away.

彼の小屋が強風に吹き飛ばされたときに、彼は足を怪我した。

- □ hurt［動］〜を傷つける、〜に怪我をさせる
- □ blow away　〜を吹き飛ばす
- □ hut［名］小屋

track 87 絵を見ながら **Listen to the English!**
発音やつづりが似た単語を、まとめて体で覚えよう！

解説は次ページ

345 invent　invest

346 do　outdo

347 vow　low

348 few　curfew

Day10

invent, invest / do, outdo / vow, low / few, curfew

345 invent [invént] | invest [invést]

Once you invent a handheld model, a lot of people will invest in your company.

コンパクトなモデルを発明したら、多くの人があなたの会社に投資するでしょう。

- □ once［接］ひとたび（…すれば）
- □ invent［動］〜を発明する
- □ handheld［形］手で持てる大きさの
- □ invest［動］投資する

346 do [dúː] | outdo [àutdúː]

I do believe the newcomer is outdoing the old hands.

あの新人はベテラン勢をしのいでいると、私は信じている。

- □ do［助動］本当に
- □ outdo［動］〜にまさる
- □ newcomer［名］新人
- □ old hand　ベテラン、熟練者

347 vow [váu] | low [lóu]

The prime minister vowed to improve the quality of life of low-income families.

首相は低所得家庭の生活の質を上げることを公約した。

- □ vow［動］〜を誓う、名言する
- □ quality of life　生活の質、QOL
- □ improve［動］〜を改善する
- □ low-income［形］低所得の

348 few [fjúː] | curfew [kɔ́ːrfjuː]

Few people support having a curfew on kids.

子どもの夜間外出禁止令に賛成する人はあまりいない。

- □ few［形］少ない、少数の
- □ support［動］〜を支持する
- □ curfew［名］夜間外出禁止令（You mustn't go out during the *curfew*. 外出禁止令が出ている間は外に出てはならない）

track 88 絵を見ながら Listen to the English!
発音やつづりが似た単語を、まとめて体で覚えよう！

解説は次ページ

349 congratulate　graduate

350 itch　pitch

351 grave　engrave

352 gross　engross

congratulate, graduate / itch, pitch / grave, engrave / gross, engross

349 congratulate [kəngrǽtʃulèit] | graduate [grǽdʒuèit]

We all congratulated him when he graduated from college.

彼が大学を卒業したとき、私たちは皆で祝いの言葉を述べた。

- □ congratulate［動］(人に) お祝いを言う
- □ graduate［動］卒業する
- □ college［名］大学、専門学校

350 itch [ítʃ] | pitch [pítʃ]

I'm itching to pitch that noisy group out of our club.

あのうるさい連中を、うちのクラブから追い出したくてしかたないんだ。

- □ itch［動］うずうずする / □ be itching to do 〜したくてたまらない
- □ pitch［動］(人を) 放り出す、〜を投げる (He *pitched* the letter into the fire. 彼はその手紙を火の中に投げ捨てた)
- □ noisy［形］やかましい

351 grave [gréiv] | engrave [ingréiv]

He'd turn in his grave if he could read the poem engraved on his gravestone.

彼が自分の墓石に刻まれた詩を読んだら、草葉の陰で嘆くだろうな。

- □ grave［名］墓 / □ turn in one's grave 草葉の陰で嘆く
- □ engrave［動］〜を刻む、彫り込む
- □ gravestone［名］墓石

352 gross [gróus] | engross [ingróus]

This gross story is actually quite engrossing.

この気持ち悪い話は本当はとても魅力的なの。

- □ gross［形］いやな、気持ち悪い
- □ actually［副］実際に、現実に
- □ engrossing［形］心を奪う、夢中にする

絵を見ながら **Listen to the English!**
発音やつづりが似た単語を、まとめて体で覚えよう！

解説は次ページ

353 enhance　hence

354 rough　enough

355 jackpot　pot

356 riddle　griddle

enhance, hence / rough, enough / jackpot, pot / riddle, griddle

353 enhance [inhæns | -hɑ́ːns] | hence [héns]

The beauty of the house was greatly enhanced by the new garden; hence we now call it the Garden House.

この家の美しさは新しい庭で飛躍的に増した。だから僕たちは今ではガーデン・ハウスと呼んでいるんだ。

- □ enhance［動］〜を高める、増進する
- □ hence［副］だから、したがって

354 rough [rʌ́f] | enough [inʌ́f]

It's only a rough translation as I didn't have enough time to do a thorough job.

完ぺきにやるには時間が足りず、粗い翻訳になっている。

- □ rough［形］大ざっぱな
- □ enough［形］十分な
- □ translation［名］翻訳
- □ thorough［形］徹底的な

355 jackpot [dʒǽkpɑ̀t] | pot [pɑ́t]

Jack hit the jackpot, so now he's got pots of money.

ジャックは大当たりしたから、今はたくさん金を持っているよ。

- □ jackpot［名］（金銭的な）大成功 / □ hit the jackpot 大当たりする
- □ pots of money 大金

356 riddle [rídl] | griddle [grídl]

It is quite a riddle how she can make such tasty griddle cakes.

彼女がどうやってあんなにおいしいホットケーキを作れるのか本当に謎だ。

- □ riddle［名］謎、難問
- □ tasty［形］おいしい
- □ griddle［名］フライパン / □ griddle cake ホットケーキ

絵を見ながら **Listen to the English!**
発音やつづりが似た単語を、まとめて体で覚えよう！

解説は次ページ

357 main　remain

358 amass　mass

359 mayor　major

360 maternal　paternal

main, remain / amass, mass / mayor, major / maternal, paternal

357 main [méin] | remain [riméin]

His main point was that a handful of people become rich while others remain poor.

一握りの人々が裕福になる一方で、残りは貧しいままだというのが彼の主張の要点だった。

- □ main［形］主な／□ main point［名］要点
- □ a handful of　一握りの
- □ remain［動］依然として〜のままである

358 amass [əmǽs] | mass [mǽs]

To get a conviction, we have to amass a mass of evidence.

有罪判決のためには、多くの証拠を積み上げなければなりません。

- □ conviction［名］有罪判決　　□ amass［動］〜を集める
- □ mass［名］多数／□ a mass of　多量の〜
- □ evidence［名］証拠

359 mayor [méiər | mέə] | major [méidʒər]

Can you believe she is the mayor of a major city?

彼女が主要都市の市長だって信じられる？

- □ mayor［名］市長
- □ major［形］主要な

360 maternal [mətə́ːrnl] | paternal [pətə́ːrnl]

My maternal grandpa showered my mother with lots of paternal love.

母方のおじいちゃんは、父親としての愛情を母にたっぷり注いだの。

- □ maternal［形］母方の　　□ grandpa［名］おじいちゃん
- □ shower［動］（人に）注ぐ　□ paternal［形］父の、父親らしい

INDEX & 単語チェック表

取り上げた単語を、本書で使われた意味とともにまとめてあります。
覚えた単語をチェックしていきましょう（右の数字はページを示しています）。

A

- [ ] a handful of 一握りの　214
- [ ] abdicate ［動］放棄する　184
  - [ ] abdicate the throne （王が）退位する
- [ ] ability ［名］能力、才能　80
- [ ] absolutely ［副］完全に、まったく　118, 162
- [ ] accent ［名］なまり、アクセント　58
- [ ] accepted ［形］一般に認められた　100
- [ ] access ［動］～にアクセスする、接近する　126
- [ ] accompany ［動］～に同行する、付き添う　88
- [ ] according to ～によると　204
- [ ] accordion ［名］《楽器》アコーディオン　204
- [ ] account ［名］勘定　68
- [ ] accredit ［動］～を認可する　100
  - [ ] accredited ［形］認可された
- [ ] actually ［副］実際に、現実に　210
- [ ] adapt ［動］順応する　22
- [ ] admission ［名］入ること、入場　30
- [ ] adopt ［動］～を養子にする　22
- [ ] adventure ［名］冒険　82
- [ ] adverse ［形］不都合な　92
- [ ] advertise ［動］（求人）広告を出す　92
- [ ] affect ［動］～に影響を及ぼす　92, 106
- [ ] affirm ［動］～を断言する、主張する　106
- [ ] afflict ［動］～を苦しめる、悩ます　106
- [ ] affluent ［形］豊かな、裕福な　106
- [ ] afloat ［副］浮かんだ、漂って　108
- [ ] agreement ［名］同意、合意　202
- [ ] aid ［名］援助、救助　38
- [ ] aide ［名］補佐官、側近　38
- [ ] alien woker 外国人労働者　192
- [ ] align oneself with ～と提携する　192
- [ ] all of a sudden 突然　148
- [ ] altitude ［名］高さ、標高　186
  - [ ] social altitude 社会的地位の高さ
- [ ] amass ［動］～を集める　214
- [ ] amazement ［名］驚き　174
- [ ] ambush ［動］～を待ち伏せして攻撃する　60
- [ ] angle ［名］観点、角度　132
  - [ ] from the angle of ～の観点から
- [ ] angry ［形］腹を立てた　180
- [ ] appetite ［名］食欲　110
- [ ] appreciate ［動］～に感謝する　128, 150
- [ ] appropriate ［形］ふさわしい、適切な　150
- [ ] are ［動］be の二人称単数および、各人称複数の現在形　98
- [ ] argument ［名］議論、主張　160
- [ ] armed ［形］武装した　106
- [ ] armor ［名］よろい　18
- [ ] arrest ［動］～を逮捕する　60
- [ ] ask ［動］～を尋ねる　48
- [ ] assent to ～に同意する、賛成する　172
- [ ] assert ［動］～を断言する、力説する　164
- [ ] assess ［動］～を評価する、査定する　126
- [ ] asset ［名］資産、財産　54
- [ ] assignment ［名］課題、任務　202
- [ ] assure ［動］（人に）～であると断言する、～を保証する　46
- [ ] athlete ［名］運動選手　90
- [ ] attempt ［動］～を試みる、企てる　122
- [ ] attention ［名］注意　134, 160
  - [ ] pay attention to ～に注意を払う
- [ ] attitude ［名］態度、姿勢　184, 186
- [ ] attribute A to B AをBのおかげだと考える　168
- [ ] audit ［動］（会計を）検査をする　54
  - [ ] auditor ［名］会計検査官
- [ ] aunt ［名］おば　88
- [ ] avenue ［名］大通り　162
- [ ] average ［形］平均の　172

B

- [ ] baby boom ベビーブーム　114
- [ ] back ［副］戻って　78
- [ ] backfire ［動］～が裏目に出る　122
- [ ] backpack ［名］リュックサック　78
  - [ ] backpacker ［名］バックパッカー（リュックを背負って旅する人）
- [ ] backward(s) ［副］後方へ　80
- [ ] bacteria ［名］バクテリア、細菌　146
- [ ] bad ［形］悪い、よくない　134
- [ ] bag ［名］かばん、バッグ　104, 124
- [ ] bail out （船から水を）かき出す　108
  - [ ] bail ... out （人を）保釈してもらう　154
- [ ] bald ［形］はげた、（タイヤが）すり減った　134
- [ ] ball ［名］球、ボール、舞踏会　172, 180
- [ ] ban ［動］～を禁止する　28, 166
- [ ] bank ［名］銀行　98
- [ ] banner ［名］横断幕、垂れ幕　28
- [ ] bare ［動］～をあらわにする　180
  - [ ] bare one's teeth 歯をむき出す
- [ ] bare ［形］裸の、むきだしの　114, 170
  - [ ] bare eyes 裸眼
  - [ ] bare feet 裸足
  - [ ] bare hands 素手
- [ ] barely ［副］かろうじて、ほとんど～ない　140
- [ ] barrow ［名］一輪手押し車　180
- [ ] bash ［動］～をぶん殴る　152
  - [ ] bash one's head against ～に頭をぶつける
- [ ] bask ［動］日光に当たる、日光浴をする　48
- [ ] batter ［動］～を連打する　34
  - [ ] battered ［形］傷んだ、ボロボロの
- [ ] battery ［名］バッテリー、電池　34
- [ ] bawl ［動］大声で叫ぶ、泣く　180
- [ ] be able to ～することができる　58
- [ ] be bound to きっと～する　46, 104
- [ ] be capable of ～の能力がある　26
- [ ] be defeated 敗北する　112
- [ ] be entitled to ～する資格がある　188

- be expected to 〜と期待されている 144
- be fagged out くたくたに疲れている、へとへとになる 70
- be governed by 〜に支配される、管理される 142
- be off one's nut 正気でない、混乱している 206
- be short of 〜が不足している 24
- beach [名]海辺、浜 48
- bead [名]ビーズ、《~s》ビーズのネックレス 44
- beam [動]微笑む、光を放つ 26
- bean [名]豆 26
  - bean curd 豆腐 120
- bear [名]クマ 180
- bear [動]〜に耐える 178
- beast [名]獣、動物 58
- beat [動]〜をやっつける、殴打する 58
- beauty [名]美人、美女 28
- beg [動](人に)〜を乞う、ねだる 104
- beggar [名]物ごい 142
- bell [名]ベル、鐘 98, 172
  - a dinner bell 食事を知らせる鐘
- belle [名]美人 172
- belly [名]腹、胃 98
  - have a full belly 満腹だ
  - have an empty belly 空腹だ
- bend [動]〜を曲げる 80
- bid [名](〜のための)努力、入札 164
  - make a bid for 〜のための努力をする
- bide [動]〜を待つ 164
  - bide one's time 好機を待つ
- black [形]黒い 48
- bland [形]味の薄い、味気ない 32
- blank [形]空虚な、白紙の 32
- blanket [名]毛布 204
- blare [名](らっぱなどの)騒々しい音 178
- bleach [動]〜を色あせさせる、漂白する 48
- bleak [形](見通しなどが)暗い 50
- blind [形]目の不自由な 22
- blink [動]まばたきする 22
- blood vessel 血管 74
- bloom [動]咲く、開花する 194
- blow away 〜を吹き飛ばす 206
- blown [形](ヒューズが)とんだ 138
- boast [動]自慢する 90
  - boaster [名]自慢する人
- book [名]本、書物 186
- boon [名]恩恵 114
- booster [名]助力となるもの、補助推進ロケット 90, 192
- booty [名]戦利品、獲物 118
- bore [動](人を)退屈させる 132
  - boring [形]退屈な
- borrow [動]〜を借りる 180
- botch [動]〜をしくじる、台無しにする 82
- both [副]両方ともに 82
- bottom [名]下部、底 64
  - Bottoms up. 乾杯!
- bow [動]おじぎをする、会釈する 54
- boxing glove ボクシング用のグラブ 148
- bracket [名]括弧 204
- branch [名]支店、部門、枝 60
- brass band ブラスバンド、吹奏楽団 178

- bread [名]パン 44
- break [動]〜を終わらせる 50
- breath [名]呼吸 160
  - hold one's breath 息を止める
- breathe [動]呼吸する 160
- breed [動]繁殖する、〜を引き起こす 26, 154
- brick [名]レンガ 44
- brief [形]短時間の、簡潔な 86
- briefcase [名]ブリーフケース、書類かばん 102
- brood [名]一かえりのひな、一腹の子 26
- brook [動]〜を我慢する、忍ぶ 108
- broom [名]ほうき 194
- buck [名]ドル、金、ポーカーの札 30, 104
  - pass the buck 責任を転嫁する
- buckle up シートベルトを締める 104
- budget [動]〜の予算を組む 182
- bug [名]虫、昆虫 68
- bulb [名]電球、白熱灯 30
  - light bulb 電球
- bulk [名]大量 30
  - in bulk まとめて
- bull [名]雄牛 132
- bullet [名]弾丸、銃弾 68
- bump [動]ぶつかる、衝突する 88, 190
  - bump into 〜と衝突する
- bumper [名]バンパー、緩衝装置 88
- burst [動]破裂する、爆発する 178
- bush [名]低木、茂み 60
- bus [名]バス 28, 38, 178
- bust [名]胸部、バスト 28
- busted [形]壊れた 178
- butter [動]〜にバターを塗る 206
- button [名]ボタン 64
  - button up ボタンをとめる、黙る

C

- camel [名]ラクダ 150
- camp [動]テントを張る、野営する 18
- can [助動]〜できる 114
- candid [形]率直な、公正な 184
- candidate [名]候補者 184
- capability [名]能力、才能 188
- capacity [名]生産能力、性能 188
- cape [名]ケープ、袖なしの肩マント 42
- card game トランプゲーム 198
- care [名]世話 202
  - take care of 〜の面倒をみる
- cash [名]現金 152
- cast [動]〜を投げる、ほうる 28
- castle [名]城、城郭 28
- cater [動]〜に料理などを提供する 58
- cave [名]洞くつ、ほら穴 52
- cease [動]〜を止める、中止する 32
  - cease fire 停戦する
- central database 中央のデータベース 126
- chant [動]歌う、詠唱する 188
- chapter [名]章 144
- charge [名]料金、使用料 204
- chase [動]〜を追いかける 144
- chaste [形]貞淑な、純潔な 144
- cheek [名]ほお 170

- □ chic ［形］しゃれた、粋な　170
- □ chick ［名］ひよこ　170
- □ chink ［名］裂け目、割れ目　18
- □ chop ［動］たたき切る　92
  - □ chop out a space for
    （木を）切って〜のためのスペースを作る
- □ chopper ［名］ヘリコプター、切る人　92
- □ chuck ［動］〜をほうる、軽く投げる　128
- □ claim ［動］〜を主張する　188
- □ clamber ［動］よじ登る、はい上がる　38
- □ clash ［名］衝突、戦闘　24
- □ click ［動］クリックする、（ボタンを）カチッと押す　64
- □ clue ［名］（問題を解く）手がかり、ヒント　94
- □ coal ［名］石炭　26
- □ cockeyed ［形］ばかな、斜視の　206
- □ collaborate with （敵側に）協力する、
  （人）と共同で行う　124
- □ collapse ［動］つぶれる、崩壊する　178
- □ colleague ［名］同僚　112
- □ college ［名］大学、専門学校　210
- □ colonel ［名］大佐　18
- □ comb ［名］くし　86
- □ compact ［形］小さくて携帯しやすい　104
- □ compel ［動］（人に）無理に〜させる　202
  - □ be compelled to 〜せざるを得ない
- □ competition ［名］競争、競技会、コンペ　102
- □ complement ［動］〜を補完する、引き立たせる　158
- □ complete ［動］〜を完了する、
  〜を完成する　144, 202
- □ complex ［形］入り組んだ、複雑な　134, 162
- □ compliment ［名］ほめ言葉、お世辞　158
  - □ fish for compliment
    相手にお世辞を言わせようとする
- □ compose ［動］〜を作曲する、構成する　54
- □ compound ［形］複数の部分からなる　186
  - □ compound interest （単利に対して）複利
- □ compulsion ［名］衝動、強制　142
- □ conceited ［形］うぬぼれた、思い上がった　198
- □ conceive ［動］（計画などを）思いつく、
  （考えなどを）抱く　62
- □ concentration ［名］集中力、専念　178
- □ concert ［名］音楽会、コンサート　198
- □ conduct ... around （人を）案内する　78
- □ confide ［動］秘密を打ち明ける　188
  - □ confide in 〜を信用して秘密を打ち明ける　74
- □ confidence ［名］信頼、自信　74
- □ confine ［動］〜を制限する　188
  - □ confined to bed 病床にある
- □ confirm ［動］〜を確認する、立証する　84, 106
  - □ confirmation ［名］確認、確証
- □ conflict ［名］闘争、衝突　106
- □ conform ［動］従う、適合する、一致する　84
- □ conformation ［名］適合、一致　84
  - □ be in conformation with 〜にかなって
- □ congratulate ［動］（人に）お祝いを言う　210
- □ conscience ［名］良心、道徳心　90
- □ conscious ［形］意識した、重視した　90
  - □ money-conscious 金銭に対する執着が強い
- □ consent ［動］同意する、応じる　172
- □ consequently ［副］結果的に　162
- □ conserve ［動］（自然などを）保護する　152
- □ constitution ［名］憲法、規約　142
- □ constrict ［動］〜を収縮させる、締めつける　74
  - □ constricted ［形］抑制された
- □ construct ［動］〜を組み立てる、建設する　74
- □ contention ［名］主張、論争　154
- □ contractor ［名］請け負い業者　118
- □ convert ［動］〜を変化させる、変換する　26
- □ conviction ［名］有罪判決　214
- □ cook ［名］料理人、コック　42
- □ cord skirt コーデュロイのスカート　172
- □ core ［名］芯　172
- □ corrupt ［形］腐敗した、堕落した　60
- □ cost ［名］費用　46
- □ cough ［名］咳　74
  - □ catch a cough 咳の風邪をひく
- □ coy ［形］にかんだ、恥ずかしそうな、純情ぶった　118
- □ cozy ［形］居心地のよい　170
- □ crack ［名］割れ目、ひび　70
- □ craft ［名］船、飛行機、航空機　38
  - □ rescue craft 救助船
- □ cram ［動］〜を詰め込む、押し込む　104
- □ cramped ［形］狭苦しい、窮屈な　104
- □ crash ［動］（自動車などを）ぶつける、
  〜をつぶす　24, 200
- □ crawl ［動］腹ばいで進む、はう　42
- □ cream ［名］クリーム　148
- □ create ［動］〜を作る、創造する　148
- □ credit ［名］名誉、信用、履修単位　100, 174
- □ creed ［名］信条、主義　154
- □ criteria ［名］判断基準　146
- □ criticize ... for …を〜の理由で批判する　72
- □ crook ［名］いかさま師、悪党、泥棒　42, 108
- □ crossword ［名］クロスワードパズル　102
- □ crow ［名］カラス ［動］鳴く　120
- □ crowd ［動］群がる、押し寄せる　120
- □ crumb ［名］（パンなどの）かけら、くず　112
- □ crumble ［動］〜を粉々にする、砕く　112
- □ cuddle ［動］〜を抱きしめる　194
- □ curb ［動］〜を抑制する、抑える　110, 120
- □ cure ［名］治療（法）　202
- □ curfew ［名］夜間外出禁止令　208
- □ curl ［動］（髪を）カールさせる、巻き毛にする　110
- □ currency ［名］通貨、貨幣　100
- □ curse ［名］ののしり　94
- □ customer ［名］顧客　200

D

- □ dab ［動］〜を軽く塗る、軽くたたく　138
- □ dad ［名］お父さん　138
- □ daft ［形］ばかげた、気のふれた　160
- □ damp ［形］湿った　18
- □ dare ［助動］思い切って…する　72
- □ dash ［動］突進する　152
- □ date ［名］ナツメヤシの実　138
- □ date ［名］デートの相手　184
- □ dazzling ［形］見事な　110
- □ debit ［動］（簿記で）〜を借方に記入する　68
- □ debt ［名］借金、負債　68
- □ decant ［動］（ワインなどを）他の容器に静かに移す　110
- □ decease ［動］死亡する　32

- □ deceased　［形］死んだ、死亡した
- □ deceit　［名］だますこと、ごまかし　32
- □ decent　［形］礼儀正しい、きちんとした　32, 58, 110
- □ deck　［名］（船の）デッキ、甲板　32
- □ declare　［動］〜を明言する　118
- □ decoy　［名］おとり、おとり用の鳥の模型　40, 118
- □ decry　［動］〜をけなす、（公然と）非難する　40
- □ deduct　［動］〜を差し引く、控除する　78
- □ defend　［動］〜を守る、擁護する　206
- □ defenseless　［形］武器を持たない　106
- □ deficient　［形］不足した　98
- □ definite　［形］明確な　120
  - □ definitely　［副］間違いなく、確かに　100
- □ deflate　［動］（通貨を）収縮させる　100
- □ deform　［動］〜を変形させる、ゆがめる　100
- □ defuse　［動］（爆発物の）信管を外す、（危険を）和らげる、鎮める　78, 94
- □ degenerate into　〜へ堕落する　160
- □ delude　［動］（人に）信じ込ませる、（人を）騙す　168
  - □ delude oneself　思い違いをする
- □ demonstrator　［名］デモの参加者　38
- □ deny　［動］〜を否定する　124
- □ depreciate　［動］価値が下がる　128
- □ desert　［動］〜から去る、〜を見捨てる　164
- □ deserve　［動］〜を受けるに値する　152
- □ desire　［名］欲望、願望　110
- □ despise　［動］〜を軽蔑する、嫌悪する　32
- □ despite　［前］〜にもかかわらず　66, 144
- □ dessert　［名］デザート　164
- □ destroy　［動］〜を破壊する　88
- □ detractor　［名］中傷する人　118
- □ diameter　［名］直径　172
- □ dictate　［動］〜を命令する　128
- □ direct　［形］一直線の、まっすぐな　166
- □ disaster　［名］災害、大惨事　140
- □ discontinue　［動］〜をやめる　102
- □ discover　［動］〜を発見する　152
- □ discredit　［動］〜の信用を傷つける　174
- □ disinterest　［名］無関心　150
  - □ disinterested　［形］関心のない
- □ dispute　［名］論争、議論　178
- □ disrepute　［目］悪評、不名誉　178
  - □ bring … into disrepute　…に悪評をもたらす
- □ dissect　［動］〜を解剖する、細かく調べる　158
- □ distillation　［名］蒸留　146
  - □ distillation plant　蒸留施設
- □ distinct　［形］明瞭な、はっきりと認識できる　24
- □ distribute　［動］〜を分配する、〜を配布する　168
- □ district　［名］地域、地方　94
- □ ditch　［名］溝、どぶ　84
- □ dive　［動］潜水する、ダイビングする　160
- □ divert　［動］〜をそらす　160
  - □ divert one's attention　（人の）注意をそらす
- □ diver　［名］水に潜る人、ダイバー　160
- □ divest　［動］〜を剥奪する　152
- □ division　［名］部門　140
- □ divorced　［形］離婚した　94
- □ dizzy　［形］目が回る、くらくらする　110
- □ do　［助動］本当に　208
- □ donate　［動］〜を提供する、贈与する　152
- □ double　［動］〜を倍にする　188, 198
- □ doubt　［動］〜を疑問に思う　198
- □ dove　［名］ハト、柔和な人　148
- □ draft　［名］風　24
  - □ draft horse　荷車を引く馬
- □ driveway　［名］（道路から家の車庫への）私道　66
- □ drought　［名］日照り、干ばつ　24
- □ dubiously　［副］半信半疑に　206
- □ duck　［名］カモ、アヒル　32
- □ duck　［動］ひょいとかがむ、ひょいと頭を下げる　128
- □ dumb　［形］頭の悪い、まぬけな　66
- □ dump　［動］〜をどさっと降ろす、（恋人を）振る　66, 190
  - □ dump truck　ダンプカー
- □ duplex　［名］複層式アパート、2世帯住宅　134

E

- □ edge　［名］端、ふち　88, 144
- □ edit　［動］〜を編集する　54
  - □ editor　［名］編集者、編集長
- □ eel　［名］ウナギ　28
- □ effect　［名］効果、結果、影響　106, 114
  - □ effective　［形］効果的な　78
- □ efficient　［形］効力のある　98
- □ elaborate　［形］念入りな、精密な　124
- □ elbow　［動］〜をひじで押す　54
  - □ elbow … out of the way　ひじで（人を）押しのける
- □ elude　［動］〜を回避する　168
- □ emergency　［名］緊急事態　80
- □ emit　［動］（声などを）発する　94
- □ emperor　［名］皇帝、帝王　20
- □ empire　［名］帝国　20
- □ employ　［動］〜（人を）雇う　118
- □ enchant　［動］〜を魅了する　188
  - □ enchanting　［形］魅惑的な
- □ engrave　［動］〜を刻む、彫り込む　210
- □ engrossing　［形］心を奪う、夢中にする　210
- □ enhance　［動］〜を高める、増進する　212
- □ enough　［形］十分な　212
- □ ensure　［動］〜を確実にする、確保する、保証する　140
- □ envoy　［名］使節、外交官　34
- □ envy　［動］〜をうらやむ、ねたむ　34
- □ err　［動］間違う、誤る　140
- □ error　［名］間違い、過失　140
- □ erupt　［動］（暴動などが）勃発する　60
- □ escape　［動］逃げる、脱出する　142
- □ estimate　［動］〜を見積もる　186
- □ evacuate　［動］〜を避難させる　80, 150
- □ evade　［動］〜を逃れる、避ける　34
- □ evaluate　［動］〜を評価する、査定する　80, 150
- □ eventually　［副］結局は、やがて　182
- □ evidence　［名］証拠　214
- □ evil　［形］邪悪な、有害な　58
- □ evolve　［動］〜を発展させる　182
- □ excess　［名］過度、過剰　126
  - □ to excess　過度に
- □ exclusive　［形］高級な、限定された　158
- □ exclude　［動］〜を除く　154
  - □ excluding　［前］〜を除いて
- □ excursion　［名］小旅行　190
- □ excuse me　すみません　158
- □ execute　［動］〜を実行する　80

218

☐ executive ［名］経営幹部、重役	80
☐ expanse ［名］広がり、（空や大地などの）広い空間	62
☐ expense ［名］費用、支出	62
☐ expert ［名］専門家	158
☐ expertise ［名］専門的知識	158
☐ explain ［動］〜を説明する	170
☐ explicit ［形］明確な	92
☐ export ［名］輸出　［動］〜を輸出する	140
☐ express mail　速達便	46
☐ expression ［名］表情、表現	130
☐ extension ［名］建て増し、延長	166
☐ extinct ［形］絶滅した	66
☐ extracurricular activity　課外活動、部活	140
☐ eye ［動］〜をじっと見る	206

F

☐ fabricate ［動］（話を）作り上げる	64
☐ face ［動］〜に直面する	164
☐ fag ［名］巻きタバコ	104
☐ fail ［動］失敗する	182
☐ fair treatment　公正な扱い	192
☐ fan ［名］扇子	194
☐ fancy ［形］しゃれた、凝った	194
☐ fate ［名］運命、運	162
☐ favorite ［形］お気に入りの	174
☐ feasibility ［名］実現可能性	164
☐ feasibility study　予備調査	
☐ feast ［名］饗宴、ごちそう	58
☐ feast ［動］ぜいたくに食べる	
☐ feat ［名］手柄、功績	58
☐ fee ［名］手数料、費用	182
☐ fence ［名］塀、さく	128
☐ fete ［名］祭典	162
☐ few ［形］少ない、少数の	208
☐ figure ［名］数字	70
☐ filthy ［形］汚い、汚れた	84
☐ find ［動］〜を見つける	18
☐ find out　気がつく、発見する	60
☐ fine ［名］〜に罰金を科する	18, 104
☐ firm ［形］断固たる、力強い	86
☐ flag ［名］旗	70
☐ flake ［名］（雪・羽毛などの）一片	200
☐ flank ［名］側面	112
☐ flash ［動］ピカッと光る、点滅する	40
☐ flask ［名］フラスコ、瓶、〈英〉魔法瓶	40
☐ flatten ［動］〜をがっかりさせる、平らにする	168
☐ flatter ［動］〜にお世辞を言う	168
☐ flee ［動］逃げる、すばやく動く	50
☐ fleet ［名］艦隊、海軍	50
☐ flexibility ［名］柔軟性	164
☐ flick ［動］（ほこり、虫などを）払い落とす	46
☐ flick through　（本などを）パラパラめくる	
☐ fling ［動］〜を投げつける、放り出す	38
☐ flint ［名］火打ち石	38
☐ float ［動］漂う、流れる	108
☐ flout ［動］（規則などを）ばかにして従わない	20
☐ fluent ［形］流暢な	106
☐ fluke ［名］まぐれ、フロック	82
☐ flunk out　（成績不良で）退学になる	82
☐ flutter ［動］〜をはためかす	168
☐ flutter one's eye lashes　ウインクする	

☐ foggy ［形］霧の深い、ぼんやりした	122
☐ haven't the foggiest idea　見当もつかない	
☐ fogy ［名］時代遅れの頑固者	122
☐ fold ［動］〜を組む、折る	174
☐ folk ［形］民間の、民俗の	174
☐ folk song　民謡、フォークソング	
☐ fool ［名］ばか者	206
☐ force … to do　…に無理に〜させる	130
☐ forward(s) ［副］前方へ	80
☐ fount ［名］源、源泉	60
☐ fraction ［名］分数	146
☐ frank ［形］率直な	112
☐ to be frank　率直に言って	
☐ French ［名］フランス語	106
☐ friction ［名］抵抗、摩擦、不和	146
☐ fridge ［名］冷蔵庫	70
☐ frill ［名］余分なもの、余計な飾り	22
☐ with no frills　余計なサービスを省いた	
☐ fringe benefit　給与外の諸手当	122
☐ fudge ［動］〜をごまかす、でっち上げる	70
☐ fumble ［動］（不器用に）手探りする	102, 148
☐ fun ［名］楽しみ	92
☐ funky ［形］ファンキーな、いかす	92
☐ funky music　黒人的なブルースやゴスペルの影響を受けた音楽	
☐ fur ［名］毛皮	72
☐ fury ［名］激怒、憤慨	72
☐ fly into a fury　烈火のごとく怒る	
☐ fuse ［名］電気ヒューズ、導火線、（爆弾などの）信管	78, 94, 138
☐ fuss ［動］やきもきする、騒ぐ	138
☐ fussy ［形］小うるさい、気難しい	42
☐ fuzzy ［形］ファジーな、不明瞭な	42

G

☐ gabble ［動］早口にしゃべる	190
☐ gabled ［形］切り妻造りの	190
☐ gal ［名］女の子、少女	130
☐ gamble away　〜を賭け事で失う	198
☐ gap ［名］割れ目、穴	128
☐ gape ［動］口をぽかんとあけて見る	128
☐ gasp ［動］あえぐ、ハッと息をのむ	174
☐ gate ［名］門、入り口	184
☐ gaze ［名］凝視、じっと見つめること	72
☐ generate ［動］〜を引き起こす	160
☐ gesture ［名］身ぶり、しぐさ	132
☐ get … to　（人を）〜に運ぶ	204
☐ get to sleep　眠りにつく	192
☐ gift ［名］贈り物	194
☐ gifted ［形］すぐれた才能のある	
☐ gist ［名］要点、骨子	194
☐ glacier ［名］氷河	88
☐ glower at　〜をにらみつける	82
☐ glue ［名］接着剤、のり	94
☐ glum ［形］陰気な、落胆した	132
☐ go bankrupt　破産する	162
☐ go bust　倒産する、つぶれる	38
☐ go out of one's way　自分の道からそれる	34
☐ goad ［動］〜を駆り立てる、刺激する	126
☐ goal ［名］目標	126
☐ gore ［動］〜を突く、突き刺す	132

☐ grade [名]成績	126
☐ graduate [動]卒業する	210
☐ grain [名]穀粒、穀物	88
☐ a grain of ほんのわずかの〜	
☐ grandpa [名]おじいちゃん	214
☐ grasp [動]〜を(しっかり)握る	174
☐ grave [名]墓	192, 210
☐ turn in one's grave 草葉の陰で嘆く	
☐ gravestone [名]墓石	210
☐ great success 大成功	198
☐ grid [名](窓などの)格子	90
☐ griddle [名]フライパン	212
☐ griddle cake ホットケーキ	
☐ grief [名]悲しみ、嘆き	86
☐ grill [動]〜を焼き網で焼く	22
☐ grin [動][名](歯を見せて)にっこりと笑う(こと)	88, 90
☐ grind [動]〜をすりつぶす、ひく	90
☐ grip [名]支配、握ること	86
☐ gripe about 〜について不平を言う	86
☐ grope one's way 手探りで進む	86
☐ gross [形]いやな、気持ち悪い	210
☐ grove [名]林、小さい森	192
☐ grumble [動]不平を言う、ぶつぶつ言う	112
☐ guarantee [動]〜を保証する	198
☐ guarantor [名]保証人	
☐ guilty [形]有罪の	164
☐ gum tree ゴムの木	132
☐ be up a gum tree 窮地に陥って	

H

☐ half [名]半分	202
☐ halve [動]〜を半分にする	202
☐ handheld [形]手で持てる大きさの	208
☐ hare [名]野ウサギ	184
☐ hat [名](縁のある)帽子	170
☐ have [動]〜を持っている	202
☐ have to 〜する必要がある	
☐ health [名]健康	200
☐ healthy [形]健康な、健康に役立つ	106
☐ healthcare [名]健康管理	122
☐ heal [動]〜を治す、癒す	180
☐ heel [名]かかと	28, 142, 180
☐ high heel ハイヒール	
☐ hell [名]地獄	144
☐ what the hell いったい	
☐ hello [名]「やあ、こんにちは」という呼びかけ	144
☐ hence [副]だから、したがって	212
☐ hepatitis [名]肝炎	110
☐ hide [動]隠れる	192
☐ hip [名]腰	166
☐ hit [動]〜にぶつかる	98
☐ hobble [動]足を引きずって歩く	112
☐ hold on power 権力にしがみつくこと	50
☐ honk [動](クラクションを)鳴らす	120
☐ hook [名]留め金	42
☐ hook [動](魚を釣り針で)釣る	72
☐ hoot [動]やじる	72
☐ horn [名]警笛、クラクション	120
☐ horrible [形]最悪な、悲惨な	112
☐ horrified [形]恐怖に襲われた	130
☐ hospitality [名]手厚いもてなし、歓待	52
☐ hostel [名]ユースホステル、簡易宿泊施設	52
☐ hostility [名]敵意、対立	52
☐ hot [形]人気のある	102
☐ hotel [名]ホテル、旅館	52
☐ huddle [動]身を寄せ合う	194
☐ hug [名][動]抱擁(する)	52, 68, 134
☐ huge [形]非常に大きい	52
☐ humble [動](人を)屈辱的な状態にする	102
☐ hump [名](ラクダなどの)背こぶ	150
☐ hurt [動]〜を傷つける、痛みを感じる	112, 154, 206
☐ hut [名]小屋	206

I

☐ ideal [形]理想的な	132
☐ idly [副]これといった目的もなく	46
☐ immigrant [名]移民、移住者	28
☐ impact [名]影響、衝撃	104
☐ impatience [名]短気、切望	132
☐ implement [動]〜を実行する	164
☐ implicit [形]暗黙の	92
☐ impression [名]印象、感動	130
☐ improve [動]〜を改善する	208
☐ impulsion [名]衝動、推進力	142
☐ in any case どんな場合でも	144
☐ in search of 〜を探し求めて	82
☐ in the dead of night 真夜中に	58
☐ inch [名]インチ	72
☐ incident [名]事件	108
☐ include [動]〜を含める	154, 190
☐ including [前]〜を含めて	
☐ income [名]所得、収入	68
☐ incursion [名]襲撃	190
☐ indeed [副]本当に	132
☐ indefinitely [副]無期限に	100
☐ indicate [動]〜を指し示す、〜を述べる	128, 184
☐ indication [名]兆候	192
☐ inert [形]自力で行動できない	174
☐ infect [動]〜に(病気を)うつす、感染させる	114
☐ infinite [形]無期限の、寛大な	120
☐ inflate [動](物価を)つり上げる	100
☐ influenced by 〜に影響される	186
☐ infringe [動](法律などを)侵害する	122
☐ infuse [動]〜を煎じる	78
☐ infusion [名]浸出、(思想などの)注入	
☐ inject [動]〜に注射する、注入する	124
☐ innocence [名]無罪	164
☐ insect [名]昆虫	158
☐ insert [動]〜に挿入する	174
☐ insist [動]〜を強く主張する	22, 30, 182
☐ insist on 〜を強く主張する	146
☐ insolent [形]横柄な、無礼な	142
☐ insolvent [形]支払い不能の	142
☐ install [動]〜を取り付ける、インストールする	70
☐ installation [名]装置、取り付け、インストール	146, 182
☐ installment [名]分割払いの1回分	182
☐ instance [名]例、場合、事実	44, 70
☐ for instance 例えば	
☐ instant [形]即席の、すぐの	70
☐ instigate [動]〜を扇動する、主導する	108
☐ instinct [名]直感、本能	24, 66

□ institution ［名］団体、機関	142
□ instruction ［名］指示、命令	92
□ insurance claim　保険金請求	186
□ intention ［名］意図、意思	154, 164, 166
□ have no intention to　〜するつもりがない	
□ interest ［名］興味	150
□ interested ［形］関心のある	
□ invade ［動］〜に侵攻する、押し寄せる	34
□ invent ［動］〜を発明する	208
□ inventor ［名］発明家、考案者	24
□ invest ［動］(〜を)投資する	152, 208
□ investor ［名］投資家	24
□ investigate ［動］〜を調査する、捜査する	108
□ involve ［動］〜を巻き込む	182
□ inward(s) ［副］内側に向けて	80
□ Irish ［形］アイルランドの	58
□ issue ［名］配給、支給	102
□ it ［代］それ	122
□ itch ［動］かゆい、うずうずする	84, 210
□ be itching to do　(〜したくて)むずむずする	

J

□ jackpot ［名］(金銭的な)大成功	212
□ hit the jackpot　大当たりする	
□ jail ［名］刑務所、留置所	154, 182
□ jangle ［動］ジャンジャン鳴る	108
□ jaunt ［名］散策、小旅行	88
□ jeopardy ［名］危険(にさらされること)	204
□ jeopardize ［動］〜を危険にさらす	
□ judge ［動］〜を判断する	146
□ jungle ［名］熱帯の密林、ジャングル	108

K

□ kernel ［名］(問題などの)核心、要点	18
□ kid ［名］子ども	124, 152
□ kidney ［名］腎臓	152
□ knee ［名］ひざ	80
□ kneel down　ひざまずく、ひざをつく	80
□ knot ［動］〜に結び目をつくる、〜を結ぶ	40
□ know ［動］〜を知っている	40

L

□ lack ［名］不足、欠如	200
□ lack ［動］(必要なものを)欠く	48
□ lad ［名］少年、若者	124
□ ladder ［名］はしご	180
□ lake ［名］湖	200
□ lamp ［名］ランプ、証明器具	18, 20
□ land ［動］(飛行機が)着陸する	92
□ land in　(悪い状況に)陥る	182
□ lanky ［形］ひょろっとした、やせこけた	98
□ lap ［名］ひざ	50
□ lapse ［名］ささいな間違い、過失	178
□ lash out at　〜を厳しく非難する	84
□ lay off　〜を一時解雇する	40
□ lead ［形］鉛の	68
□ league ［名］同盟	112
□ leak ［動］(秘密などを)漏らす、漏えいする	50
□ lease ［名］賃貸借契約	26
□ ledge ［名］出っ張り、棚、岩礁	34, 186
□ ledger ［名］台帳	34

□ legally ［副］合法的に	118
□ leisure ［形］暇な	140
□ leisure time　暇な時間	
□ leverage ［名］てこの作用	172
□ lick ［動］〜をなめる	46, 54, 64, 130
□ lick a person's boots　(人に)こびへつらう	118
□ lick one's wounds　傷を癒す	54
□ lie down on the job　仕事をおろそかにする	40
□ life raft　救命いかだ、ゴムボート	108
□ lightning ［名］稲妻、電光	40
□ lip ［名］唇	54
□ loan ［名］融資、借金、ローン	148, 198
□ local ［形］地元の	80
□ lock ［名］錠	174
□ lodge ［動］〜を提出する、申し立てる	186
□ Look!　見て、ほら	42
□ lose ［動］〜を失う、なくす	44
□ loss ［名］損失、失うこと	44, 150
□ a big loss　大きな損害、大損	
□ lot ［名］たくさん	102
□ lout ［名］無骨者	20
□ love ［動］〜が大好きである	148
□ love to　〜するのが好きである	82
□ lovely ［形］美しい、かわいらしい	58
□ low ［名］(自動車の)ローギア　［形］低い	62
□ low-income ［形］低所得の	208
□ lower ［動］〜を下げる、低くする	82
□ lubricant ［名］潤滑油、潤滑剤	146
□ lubricate ［動］〜に潤滑油を差す、〜を円滑にする	64, 146
□ luck ［名］運、成功、運命	30, 32, 114
□ lucky ［形］幸運な、運のいい	130, 138
□ lug ［動］苦労して運ぶ、引っ張りあげる	62, 64
□ lump ［名］こぶ、塊	20, 150
□ take one's lumps　罰や報いを受ける	
□ lung ［名］肺	62, 106
□ lung cancer　肺がん	
□ lurk ［動］潜む、隠れる	114

M

□ mad ［形］気が狂った	20
□ be mad with joy　狂喜する	
□ mad as a hatter　頭がすっかり狂って	126
□ main ［形］主な	214
□ main point ［名］要点	
□ major ［形］主要な	214
□ make ends meet　生活の収支を合わせる	140
□ manager ［名］支配人、経営者	98
□ mass ［名］多数	214
□ a mass of　多量の〜	
□ matador ［名］主役の闘牛士(マタドール)	132
□ maternal ［形］母方の	214
□ mayor ［名］市長	184, 214
□ maze ［名］迷路、迷宮	72
□ meal ［名］食事	206
□ medication ［名］薬物治療、投薬	192
□ merely ［副］ただ、単に	144
□ millionaire ［名］百万長者	142
□ misdirect ［動］〜に間違って教える	166
□ moan ［動］不満を言う、嘆く、うめく	148
□ monk ［名］僧	188

- motel ［名］モーテル、自動車旅行用の宿泊施設　52
- mucky ［形］じめじめした、蒸し暑い　138
- mud ［名］つまらないもの、泥　20, 42
  - One's name is mud. 〈人〉の評判が地に落ちる
- mug ［名］マグカップ、ジョッキ　134
- mulch ［名］根覆い　66
- musical composition　楽曲、音楽作品　54

N

- nab ［動］〜を取り押さえる　124
- nag at　〜に口うるさく言う　124
- near future　近い未来　184
- negotiation ［名］交渉、協議　68, 92
- neighbor ［名］隣人、近所の人　138
- newcomer ［名］新人　208
- noisy ［形］やかましい　210
- nook ［名］隅、隠れ場所　186

O

- official ［名］当局者　60
- oily ［形］油っこい　110
- old hand　ベテラン、熟練者　208
- olive ［名］オリーブ　192
- on occasion　時々　148
- on time　遅れずに、予定通りに　198
- once ［接］ひとたび（…すれば）　208
- operation ［名］手術、事業　124
- orbit ［名］軌道　90
- outcome ［名］結果、成果　68
- outdo ［動］〜にまさる　208
- output ［名］生産高　188, 198
- outward(s) ［副］外側へ　80
- overall ［形］全体の　74
- overdue ［形］期日を過ぎた、期限切れの　18

P

- pack ［動］〜を詰め込む　78
  - pack up　荷物をまとめる　48
- pal ［名］仲間、友達　130
- parapet ［名］胸壁、（屋根などの）手すり　28
- paternal ［形］父の、父親らしい　214
- patient ［形］忍耐強い　184
- patio ［名］テラス、中庭　190
- pay up　借金を全額払う　68
- pellet ［名］小球、錠剤　68
- per annum　1年につき　186
- perceive ［動］（感覚で）〜に気づく　62
- permission ［名］許可、承認　30
- perplex ［動］〜を当惑させる　162
- persist in　〜に固執する　30
- pick up　〜を持ち上げる、車で迎えに行く　44, 48
- pile ［名］大量、積み重ね　190
- pinch ［動］〜を盗む、掠め取りする　72
- pitch ［動］（人を）放り出す、〜を投げる　210
- plain ［形］平原、平野　170
- play with　〜で遊ぶ　166
- pleasure ［名］喜び、楽しさ　120
- plenty of　たくさんの〜　158
- policy ［名］方針、政策　84
- pose ［動］（問題などを）引き起こす　46
- possibility ［名］可能性　24
- post ［動］《英》〜を郵送する、投函する　46
- posture ［名］姿勢、態度　132
- pots of money　大金　212
- pound ［名］ポンド　186
- prefer ［動］〜を好む　190
- presidential ［形］大統領の　38
- privilege ［名］特権、恩恵　34
- procure ［動］〜を手に入れる　202
- profit ［名］利益　152
- property ［名］所有物、財産　160
- proposal ［名］提案、企画案、計画　172
- prospect ［名］見通し　50
- public access　公共のアクセス　126
- pull on　身に着ける　148
- purposely ［副］わざと、故意に　166
- put A above B　AをBより優先させる　200

Q

- quality of life　生活の質、QOL　208
- quickly ［副］速く、敏速に　128

R

- raft ［名］いかだ　38, 160
  - life raft　救命ボート
- ramble ［動］散歩する、ぶらつく　58
- ranch ［名］牧場、農場　60
- rare ［形］珍しい、まれな　170, 184
  - rarely ［副］めったに〜しない　140
- rave ［動］夢中になって話す　52
- raw material　原料　98
- reassure ［動］〜を安心させる、〜に再保証する　46
- rebound ［動］跳ね返る　46
- reclaim ［動］〜の返還を要求する　188
- reel ［動］ふらふらする、よろめく、動揺する　142
- reflate ［動］（通貨を）再膨張させる　100
- reform ［名］改革、改善　100
  - reform plan　改革案　182
- refrigeration ［名］冷却、冷凍　148
- refugee ［名］避難者、難民　100
- refuse ［動］〜を断る　60, 94
- reject ［動］〜を拒絶する、拒否する　124
- release ［動］〜を解放する、自由にする　26
- remain ［動］依然として〜のままである　144, 214
- remind ... that　…に〜であることを思い出させる　124
- remit ［動］（金を）送る　94
- remove ［動］〜を取り除く　78
- renege ［動］（約束を）破る　162
- repay ［動］（金を）返す　198
- repetition ［名］繰り返し　102
- replete with　〜に満ちた、〜で一杯の　144
- reputation ［名］評判、名声　174, 204
- research ［名］研究、調査　128
- resident ［名］居住者　80, 150
- resist ［動］抵抗する　22
- resolutely ［副］決然と、断固として　118
- respite ［名］息抜き、休息　66
- restrict ［動］〜を制限する、限定する　74, 94
- retention ［名］保持、維持　134
- revert ［動］（元の状態に）戻る　26
- riddle ［名］謎、難問　212
- right ［形］適した　184

☐ robust ［形］強固な、活気のある、堅固な 38	☐ supply ［名］供給 98
☐ rock ［名］岩 172	☐ support ［動］〜を支持する 208
☐ roof rack 《英》車の屋根の上の荷台 70	☐ swap ［動］〜を交換する、取り換える 44
☐ room and board 部屋代と食事代 154	☐ swivel ［動］〜を回転させる 166
☐ rooster ［名］雄鶏 192	
☐ rope ［名］縄、ロープ 86	## T
☐ rosy ［形］血色のよい、ばら色の 170	☐ take ［動］〜を取る 42
☐ rot ［名］くだらないもの 102	☐ take someone up on （人）の〜に応じる 150
☐ rote ［名］機械的な暗記 102	☐ tangle ［動］もつれる、からまる 132
☐ learn ... by rote …を丸暗記する	☐ tariff ［名］関税、運賃 204
☐ rough ［形］大ざっぱな 212	☐ tarot ［名］タロットカード 162
☐ rove ［動］〜を流浪する、さまよう 82	☐ tasty ［形］おいしい 212
☐ rubber band 輪ゴム 166	☐ tempt ［動］〜を誘惑する 122
☐ rubbish ［名］ごみ 190	☐ territory ［名］領土、領地 72
☐ run ［動］（機械を）動かす 98	☐ thorough ［形］徹底的な 212
	☐ thrash ［動］〜を強く打つ、むち打つ 200
## S	☐ threat ［名］脅し 92
☐ salary ［名］給料 122	☐ threaten ［動］〜と脅す 50, 102
☐ scam ［名］ペテン、詐欺 114	☐ tit for tat 売り言葉に買い言葉 122
☐ scan ［動］〜をざっと見る、画像を取り込む 114, 204	☐ tomb ［名］墓 86
☐ scandal ［名］醜聞、スキャンダル 204	☐ tough ［形］強い、頑丈な 74
☐ scanner ［名］スキャナー 204	☐ translation ［名］翻訳 212
☐ scare ［動］〜を怖がらせる 202	☐ trap ［動］（人）を閉じ込める 52
☐ scared ［形］怖がる	☐ triplex ［名］3階建てアパート 134
☐ scrape off 〜をこすり落とす 42	☐ troop ［名］軍隊、中隊 60
☐ scrawl ［動］〜を走り書きする、殴り書きする 42	☐ truth ［名］事実 88
☐ seclude ［動］〜を締め出す 190	☐ tug ［名］強く引くこと 134
☐ secluded ［形］人里離れた、隠遁した	☐ tug boat えい航船、タグボート
☐ sedate ［形］落ち着いた、穏やかな 138	☐ tumble ［動］転ぶ、倒れる 148
☐ see ［動］〜が分かる 104	☐ tumble down the stairs 階段を転がり落ちる
☐ service charge サービス料、手数料 78	
☐ set out on 〜に出発する 190	## U
☐ sex ［名］性行為、性別 66	☐ urinary ［形］尿の 134
☐ shady ［形］日陰の 186	☐ utter ［形］完全な、全くの 206
☐ share ［名］株、株式 128	
☐ shatter ［動］〜を打ち砕く、粉砕する 126	## V
☐ shiny ［形］光る、輝く 44	☐ veggy ［名］野菜 130
☐ shower ［動］（人に）注ぐ 214	☐ vehicle ［名］車、車両 88
☐ shrug ［動］（肩を）すくめる 132	☐ venue ［名］現場、会場 162
☐ sink ［動］〜を沈める 18	☐ violence ［名］暴力、暴力行為 60
☐ skid ［動］滑る 124	☐ vision ［名］画像、映像 140
☐ slack ［形］不景気な、活気のない 200	☐ vow ［動］〜を誓う、名言する 208
☐ slap ［動］〜をひっぱたく、平手打ちにする 50	
☐ slash ［動］（予算・人員などを）大幅に削減する 84	## W
☐ sledge ［名］そり 88	☐ wall ［名］壁、塀 180
☐ slick ［形］つるつるした、口のうまい 54, 130	☐ ware ［名］商品、売品（通例 one's wares） 98
☐ slow ［副］ゆっくり、遅く 62	☐ Watch out! 危ない！ 気をつけて！ 98
☐ slug ［名］怠け者、ナメクジ 64	☐ wealth ［名］富 200
☐ snatch ［動］〜をひったくる 124	☐ wedge ［名］くさび 144
☐ so ... that 〜 あまりに…なので〜 86	☐ whip ［名］むち 166
☐ somehow ［副］どういうわけか 80	☐ crack a whip むちをピシッと鳴らす
☐ spread ［動］散らばる 178	☐ win ［動］〜を得る 74
☐ stance ［名］姿勢、立場 44	☐ wine and dine 気前よくもてなす 64
☐ starting grid スタート位置 90	☐ wisdom ［名］英知、知恵 60
☐ stride ［動］大股で歩く 90	
☐ struggle ［名］奮闘 192	## Y
☐ subsequently ［副］その後 162	☐ youth ［名］青年、若者 112
☐ subsist on 〜で生計を立てる 182	☐ yucky ［形］まずい、気持ち悪い 130
☐ sue ［動］〜を訴える、告訴する 102	
☐ suffer ［動］病気をする、苦しむ 114	## Z
☐ superintendent ［名］（組織などの）最高責任者 84	☐ Z sign Z字形の標識 62

223

ジェイミー・チェイス
Jamie Chase

1980年代後半に広州のアメリカ総領事館において通訳、翻訳業務に携わった後、90年代にオーストラリア・パース市のアレクサンダー・カレッジで英語を教える。2006年より広州のファーレン・カレッジで教鞭をとっている。中国系オーストラリア人として長年にわたって英語教育に従事し、学生たちが英語を勉強するうえで直面する問題を解決するために努めてきた。ひとりひとりの学生に合わせた、きめ細かいオーダーメイド式の指導には定評がある。本書『Lazy & Easy English』（原題）は、非英語圏の学生たちがどのようにすれば簡単に、また、効果的に英語を学習することができるかという研究の最新の成果であり、2008年に中国で出版。好評を博して2009年には韓国語版が出版された。

[CD付]
超効率的！ 笑って覚えるイラスト英単語

2011年10月20日 　　初版第1刷発行

著　者　　　ジェイミー・チェイス

発行者　　　原　雅久
発行所　　　株式会社 朝日出版社
　　　　　　〒101-0065　東京都千代田区西神田3-3-5
　　　　　　TEL: 03-3263-3321　FAX: 03-5226-9599
　　　　　　http://www.asahipress.com（PC）
　　　　　　http://asahipress.jp（ケータイ）
　　　　　　http://twitter.com/asahipress_com（ツイッター）

印刷・製本　　凸版印刷株式会社
イラスト　　　Lan Heng
装丁　　　　　今井高宏（トランスモグラフ）
ナレーション　Bianca Allen、Steven Ashton
CD録音・編集　ELEC（財団法人 英語教育協議会）
DTP・本文デザイン　メディアアート

乱丁・落丁本はお取り替えいたします。
無断で複写複製することは著作権の侵害になります。

ⓒJamie Chase and Asahi Press, 2011
ISBN978-4-255-00606-2 C0082
Printed in Japan